To the Pioneers and Innovators in Agriculture

This book is dedicated to the countless individuals who are at the forefront of transforming Indian agriculture through the integration of Artificial Intelligence. To the visionary researchers, dedicated farmers, and relentless innovators who are working tirelessly to harness the power of AI for the benefit of our agricultural sector, this work is for you.

Your passion for improving agricultural practices and your commitment to embracing new technologies inspire us all. Your efforts in bridging the gap between tradition and innovation pave the way for a more sustainable and prosperous future for Indian agriculture.

To the farmers who are adapting to these new technologies with courage and optimism, and to the researchers and practitioners who continue to explore new frontiers in AI, this book stands as a testament to your contributions and achievements.

May this work serve as a source of inspiration and a guide for future advancements in the field, driving continued progress and ensuring a brighter, more sustainable future for agriculture in India.

With deep respect and admiration,

Dr. Satwik Sahay Bisarya

Contents

Acknowledgements

Writing a book of this scope and significance is a collaborative effort, and there are many individuals and organizations whose support has been instrumental in bringing this work to fruition.

First and foremost, I would like to express my profound gratitude to the researchers, scholars, and practitioners in the field of agricultural technology and Artificial Intelligence. Your pioneering work and groundbreaking research have laid the foundation for this book and continue to drive progress in the integration of AI into agriculture.

I am deeply thankful to the farmers and agricultural experts who shared their insights and experiences. Your practical knowledge and willingness to adapt to new technologies have provided invaluable perspectives and real-world applications of AI in agriculture.

Special thanks go to the institutions and organizations that have supported this research, including the [Institution/University Name] for providing the resources and environment conducive to this study. Your commitment to advancing agricultural sciences and technologies has been a great source of inspiration.

I would also like to acknowledge the contributions of the various startups and technology companies working at the intersection of AI and agriculture.

A heartfelt thank you to my colleagues and mentors who have provided guidance, feedback, and encouragement throughout this project. Your expertise and support have been invaluable in refining the ideas and ensuring the accuracy and relevance of the content.

To my family and friends, your unwavering support and patience have been a pillar of strength throughout the writing process. Your belief in this project and in me has been a constant source of motivation.

Finally, I extend my gratitude to the readers of this book. Your interest in the role of AI in agriculture and your commitment to exploring new frontiers in farming practices are what make this endeavor meaningful.

This book is a collective effort, and its success is due to the contributions of many dedicated individuals. Thank you for your support, encouragement, and commitment to advancing agriculture through the power of Artificial Intelligence.

Dr. Satwik Sahay Bisarya

Prologue

Navigating the Future of Indian Agriculture

As dawn breaks over the vast landscapes of India, the fields stir with the promise of another productive day. For centuries, Indian agriculture has been the lifeblood of the nation, nurturing not just crops and livestock, but also the dreams and aspirations of millions. Yet, as the world evolves, so too must the ways in which we cultivate our land and manage our resources.

The advent of Artificial Intelligence (AI) has introduced a new era of possibilities, offering tools and technologies that promise to revolutionize agriculture in unprecedented ways. From precision farming and predictive analytics to smart irrigation systems and autonomous machinery, AI is poised to transform every facet of agricultural practice.

This book, "The Role of Artificial Intelligence in Indian Agriculture: Current Scenario and Future Prospects," explores the profound impact of AI on the agricultural landscape of India. It delves into the current applications of AI technologies, examines their implications for productivity and sustainability, and envisions the future of agriculture shaped by these innovations.

The journey through this book will take you from understanding the basics of AI and its historical development, to analyzing the specific challenges faced by Indian farmers and how AI can address them. We will explore the role of AI in enhancing crop management, livestock health, soil monitoring, and water resource optimization. Furthermore, we will look at how AI is influencing market dynamics and creating new opportunities for smallholder farmers.

Through a comprehensive examination of case studies, success stories, and emerging trends, this book aims to provide a holistic view of how AI is already making a difference and how it can further drive agricultural advancement in India. It will also address the barriers to AI adoption, such as technological, economic, and infrastructural challenges, and propose solutions to overcome them.

In envisioning the future, we recognize the importance of collaboration among government bodies, private sector players, and research institutions. The collective effort of these stakeholders will be crucial in realizing the full potential of AI in agriculture, ensuring that its benefits are equitably distributed and contribute to the sustainable development of the sector.

As we embark on this exploration, we invite you to consider the transformative power of AI not just as a technological marvel but as a tool for profound change. In a country where agriculture is both a livelihood and a way of life, the integration of AI offers a beacon of hope—a promise of a future where farming is more efficient, sustainable, and resilient.

May this book serve as a guide and inspiration for all those involved in the journey of modernizing Indian agriculture, fostering innovation, and building a prosperous future for our farming communities.

With anticipation for the future and respect for the past,

Dr. Satwik Sahay Bisarya

Authors' Affiliation

Dr. Satwik Sahay Bisarya, Associate Professor, Faculty of Agriculture Science, SAM Global University, Raisen, Madhya Pradesh, India

Dr. Anil Dhakad, Assistant Professor, Faculty of Agriculture Science, SAM Global University, Raisen, Madhya Pradesh, India

Dr. Priyansh Rahangdale, Assistant Professor, Faculty of Agriculture Science, SAM Global University, Raisen, Madhya Pradesh, India

CHAPTER I

Introduction to Artificial Intelligence in Agriculture

Definition of Artificial Intelligence

Artificial Intelligence (AI) refers to the simulation of human intelligence processes by machines, particularly computer systems. These processes include learning (the acquisition of information and rules for using the information), reasoning (using rules to reach approximate or definite conclusions), and self-correction. AI systems are designed to perform tasks that typically require human intelligence, such as visual perception, speech recognition, decision-making, and language translation.

AI can be broadly categorized into three types:

- **Artificial Narrow Intelligence (ANI)**: Also known as weak AI, this type of AI is designed to perform a specific task or a set of tasks. It operates under a narrow range of constraints and cannot perform tasks beyond its programming. Examples include virtual assistants like Siri or Alexa, and AI-powered recommendation systems.
- **Artificial General Intelligence (AGI)**: Also known as strong AI, AGI refers to a type of AI that possesses the ability to understand, learn, and apply knowledge across a wide range of tasks, similar to human intelligence. AGI is still theoretical and has not been realized yet.
- **Artificial Superintelligence (ASI)**: ASI is a level of intelligence that surpasses human intelligence across all fields, including creativity, problem-solving, and social intelligence. Like AGI, ASI is currently hypothetical and the subject of much debate and speculation.

Components of AI

AI is composed of several key components, each contributing to its overall functionality:

- **Machine Learning (ML)**: A subset of AI, machine learning involves the development of algorithms that allow computers to learn from and make predictions based on data. ML models improve their performance as they are exposed to more data over time.

- **Natural Language Processing (NLP)**: NLP enables computers to understand, interpret, and respond to human language in a meaningful way. This is used in applications like chatbots, translation services, and sentiment analysis.
- **Computer Vision**: This aspect of AI allows machines to interpret and make decisions based on visual data from the world. It is used in areas such as facial recognition, object detection, and autonomous vehicles.
- **Robotics**: Robotics involves the design and creation of robots that can perform tasks autonomously or semi-autonomously. AI is crucial in making these robots capable of performing complex tasks in dynamic environments.
- **Expert Systems**: These are AI programs that mimic the decision-making abilities of a human expert. They use a set of rules and knowledge bases to make decisions in specific domains, such as medical diagnosis or financial forecasting.

Scope of AI in Agriculture

The scope of AI in agriculture is vast and continually expanding as technology advances. AI's applications in agriculture include but are not limited to:

- **Precision Farming**: AI enables precision farming practices, which involve using data to optimize field-level management regarding crop farming. This includes irrigation, pesticide application, and fertilization, leading to improved yields and reduced waste.
- **Predictive Analytics**: AI-powered predictive analytics can forecast weather patterns, crop yields, and pest infestations, helping farmers make informed decisions and plan their activities more effectively.
- **Automated Machinery**: AI-driven robots and machinery can perform repetitive tasks such as planting, weeding, and harvesting, improving efficiency and reducing the need for manual labor.
- **Supply Chain Optimization**: AI can streamline the agricultural supply chain, reducing losses and ensuring that products reach markets more quickly. This includes AI-driven logistics, market price forecasting, and demand prediction.
- **Resource Management**: AI helps in the efficient management of resources such as water and energy, optimizing their use based on real-

time data and predictive models.

- **Crop Health Monitoring**: AI systems, combined with satellite imagery and drones, can monitor crop health in real-time, identifying issues such as nutrient deficiencies, disease outbreaks, or pest invasions early on.
- **Soil and Water Management**: AI can assess soil conditions and manage irrigation systems to ensure crops receive the optimal amount of water, thereby improving yields and conserving resources.

Global and Indian Context of AI in Agriculture

- **Global Perspective**: Globally, AI is transforming agriculture by enabling smarter and more sustainable farming practices. Countries like the United States, Israel, and the Netherlands are at the forefront of integrating AI with agriculture, with innovations ranging from autonomous tractors to AI-powered plant breeding.
- **Indian Context**: In India, AI in agriculture is still in its nascent stages but is rapidly gaining traction. Given India's diverse agro-climatic conditions, large farming population, and the challenges of resource management, AI has the potential to revolutionize Indian agriculture. The Indian government, private sector, and startups are increasingly investing in AI to address issues such as low productivity, resource inefficiency, and market unpredictability.

Future Prospects

The future of AI in agriculture promises further advancements and broader adoption. With continuous improvements in AI technology, we can expect:

- **Enhanced Decision-Making**: AI will provide even more accurate and actionable insights, allowing farmers to make better-informed decisions that increase productivity and sustainability.
- **Increased Automation**: As AI technology progresses, more tasks in agriculture will become automated, reducing the reliance on human labor and increasing efficiency.
- **Climate-Resilient Agriculture**: AI will play a critical role in developing and implementing farming practices that are resilient to climate change, ensuring food security in the face of environmental challenges.

- **Personalized Farming**: AI will enable highly personalized farming practices, where recommendations and interventions are tailored to individual plots, crops, and farmers, optimizing every aspect of the agricultural process.

AI is poised to play a transformative role in agriculture, particularly in a country like India, where it can address critical challenges and lead to a more sustainable and productive agricultural sector.

Historical Overview of AI in Global Agriculture

The integration of Artificial Intelligence (AI) into agriculture has been a gradual process that evolved alongside advancements in computing, data science, and machine learning. Below is an overview of the key milestones and developments in the application of AI in global agriculture.

1. Early Beginnings (1960s - 1980s)

- **Introduction of Computing in Agriculture**: The 1960s marked the beginning of digital technology in agriculture, primarily through the use of computers for data management. Early systems were basic and involved simple data collection and analysis, often for research purposes.
- **Development of Expert Systems**: In the 1970s and 1980s, expert systems were among the first AI applications in agriculture. These systems used rule-based algorithms to mimic the decision-making abilities of human experts. They were primarily used for specific tasks like crop management and pest control. One notable example was the development of **DENDRAL** and **MYCIN**, early expert systems that inspired agricultural applications.
- **Adoption of Remote Sensing**: The late 1970s also saw the introduction of remote sensing technologies, which laid the groundwork for later AI developments. Satellite imagery began to be used for large-scale monitoring of agricultural lands, particularly in developed countries.

2. The Rise of Precision Agriculture (1990s - 2000s)

- **Emergence of Precision Farming**: The 1990s marked a significant shift towards precision agriculture, an approach that leverages data and technology to optimize field-level management. Early GPS technology, combined with geographic information systems (GIS), allowed farmers to map fields and apply inputs more precisely, reducing waste and increasing efficiency.

- **Machine Learning and Data Analytics**: The rise of machine learning in the late 1990s began to influence agricultural practices. Machine learning algorithms were used to analyze large datasets from farms, helping to identify patterns and make predictions about crop yields, soil health, and pest outbreaks.
- **Automated Equipment**: During this period, the agricultural machinery industry began to incorporate early forms of AI. Tractors and harvesters were equipped with sensors and basic AI to automate certain tasks like planting, fertilizing, and harvesting.
- **Adoption of Decision Support Systems (DSS)**: DSS became popular in this era, aiding farmers in making informed decisions by analyzing environmental data and crop conditions. These systems integrated various AI components such as predictive modeling and optimization algorithms.

3. The AI Boom and Technological Integration (2010s - Present)

- **Advancements in Machine Learning and Deep Learning**: The 2010s saw an explosion in AI capabilities due to advancements in machine learning and deep learning. These technologies began to be widely applied in agriculture for tasks such as crop and soil monitoring, predictive analytics, and automated irrigation systems.
- **AI-Powered Drones and Robotics**: The integration of AI with drones and robotics revolutionized farm management. Drones equipped with AI-based imaging technology began to be used for monitoring crop health, assessing field conditions, and even applying treatments. Robots capable of performing tasks like weeding, harvesting, and planting became increasingly sophisticated.
- **Smart Farming and IoT**: The Internet of Things (IoT) began to play a crucial role in agriculture, with AI-enhanced sensors being deployed across farms to collect real-time data on soil moisture, weather conditions, and crop health. This data is used by AI algorithms to provide actionable insights and automate decision-making processes.
- **AI in Livestock Management**: AI applications expanded to livestock farming, with systems developed to monitor animal health, optimize feeding, and manage breeding programs. AI-driven cameras and sensors are now commonly used to track the behavior and condition of livestock,

ensuring better care and productivity.

- **Blockchain and AI in Supply Chain Management**: Combining blockchain technology with AI has improved traceability and transparency in the agricultural supply chain. This integration helps ensure food safety, reduce fraud, and optimize logistics.

4. Global Case Studies and Milestones

- **USA**: The United States has been a leader in the adoption of AI in agriculture. Companies like **John Deere** have integrated AI into their machinery, offering smart tractors that use AI to optimize planting and harvesting. The **FarmBeats** project by Microsoft uses AI and IoT to provide real-time farm data for decision-making.
- **Netherlands**: The Netherlands, known for its advanced agricultural practices, uses AI extensively in greenhouse management and precision farming. Dutch farms often employ AI for crop monitoring, pest detection, and yield optimization, significantly boosting productivity in a small land area.
- **Israel**: Israel has been a pioneer in the use of AI for water management, critical for its arid environment. Companies like **Taranis** and **Prospera** have developed AI solutions for precision irrigation, disease prediction, and crop management, making Israeli agriculture highly efficient.
- **China**: China has rapidly adopted AI in agriculture, focusing on automation and large-scale data analytics to manage its vast agricultural sector. AI-powered drones and robots are increasingly used in rice paddies and orchards, and AI is central to China's efforts to ensure food security.
- **India**: India has begun to see significant AI integration in agriculture, with a focus on solving local challenges such as water scarcity, pest management, and market access for smallholder farmers. Government initiatives and private startups are driving the adoption of AI in areas like predictive analytics, crop monitoring, and automated equipment.

5. Current Trends and Future Directions

- **Climate-Smart Agriculture**: AI is increasingly being applied to develop climate-smart agricultural practices, helping farmers adapt to changing weather patterns and reduce the environmental impact of farming.

- **AI in Plant Breeding**: The use of AI in genomics and plant breeding is helping to accelerate the development of new crop varieties that are more resilient to diseases and environmental stresses.
- **Integration with Big Data and Cloud Computing**: The combination of AI with big data analytics and cloud computing is enhancing the ability to process and analyze vast amounts of agricultural data, leading to more informed and timely decisions.
- **Ethical and Sustainable AI**: As AI becomes more entrenched in agriculture, there is growing emphasis on developing ethical AI systems that are sustainable and accessible to smallholder farmers, particularly in developing countries.

This historical overview underscores the transformative role that AI has played and continues to play in global agriculture. From its early beginnings in expert systems to its current application in precision farming and robotics, AI has revolutionized how food is grown, managed, and distributed, paving the way for a more efficient, sustainable, and resilient agricultural sector.

Relevance of AI in Indian Agriculture

India, with its diverse agro-climatic conditions, vast agricultural landscape, and a large population dependent on farming, stands to gain significantly from the integration of Artificial Intelligence (AI) into its agricultural practices. The relevance of AI in Indian agriculture is multifaceted, addressing critical challenges while also opening new avenues for innovation and growth.

1. Addressing Critical Challenges in Indian Agriculture

- **Smallholder Farming**: The majority of Indian farmers are smallholders, cultivating less than two hectares of land. AI can empower these farmers by providing them with precise, data-driven insights that were previously inaccessible. AI-driven tools can guide them on optimal planting times, crop choices, pest control, and resource management, leading to better yields and incomes.
- **Resource Scarcity**: Water and soil are critical but often scarce resources in Indian agriculture. AI systems, through predictive analytics and real-time monitoring, can optimize the use of water, fertilizers, and pesticides, ensuring that these resources are used efficiently. Precision agriculture techniques enabled by AI can minimize wastage, thereby

conserving water and improving soil health.

- **Climate Change and Weather Variability**: Indian agriculture is highly vulnerable to climate change and erratic weather patterns. AI can play a crucial role in providing accurate weather forecasts, early warnings about extreme weather events, and actionable insights to mitigate the effects of climate change. This can help farmers make timely decisions to protect their crops and livelihoods.

- **Pest and Disease Management**: Pests and diseases are significant threats to Indian crops, often leading to substantial losses. AI, through image recognition and machine learning, can help in the early detection of pests and diseases, allowing for prompt and targeted interventions. AI-powered apps and devices can identify issues in real-time, reducing the reliance on blanket pesticide applications.

2. Enhancing Productivity and Efficiency

- **Precision Farming**: AI facilitates precision farming, where inputs such as seeds, water, and fertilizers are applied optimally based on data analysis. This increases productivity while reducing costs and environmental impact. In a country like India, where agricultural productivity is often lower than global averages, AI-driven precision farming can significantly boost yields.

- **Yield Prediction and Crop Monitoring**: AI tools can predict crop yields more accurately by analyzing data from various sources such as satellite imagery, weather patterns, and soil health. This helps farmers and policymakers plan better, reducing the uncertainty that often plagues Indian agriculture. Continuous monitoring of crops through AI-driven drones and sensors ensures that any deviations from expected growth can be addressed promptly.

- **Supply Chain Optimization**: AI can streamline the agricultural supply chain in India by improving logistics, reducing wastage, and ensuring that produce reaches markets more efficiently. AI-powered platforms can predict demand, optimize pricing, and match supply with demand, thereby reducing the typical gluts and shortages in Indian markets.

3. Empowering Farmers through Information and Technology

- **Access to Knowledge**: AI can bridge the knowledge gap for Indian farmers by providing them with real-time, context-specific information through mobile apps and digital platforms. Farmers can receive personalized advice on crop management, market prices, weather forecasts, and best practices, all tailored to their specific conditions and needs.
- **Financial Inclusion and Risk Management**: AI can also enhance financial inclusion for farmers by improving their access to credit, insurance, and other financial services. AI algorithms can assess a farmer's creditworthiness more accurately, enabling better risk management and reducing the likelihood of defaults. AI-driven crop insurance products can offer more accurate and fair premiums based on real-time data.
- **Market Linkages**: AI can improve market access for farmers by connecting them directly with buyers through digital platforms. This reduces the reliance on middlemen, ensuring that farmers receive a fair price for their produce. AI can also help in identifying the best markets and times to sell produce, maximizing profits.

4. Supporting Sustainable Agricultural Practices

- **Climate-Smart Agriculture**: AI plays a vital role in promoting climate-smart agriculture practices in India. By analyzing vast datasets, AI can help farmers adapt to climate change by suggesting resilient crop varieties, optimal planting schedules, and efficient water management practices.
- **Reducing Environmental Impact**: AI-driven precision agriculture reduces the environmental footprint of farming by minimizing the overuse of water, fertilizers, and pesticides. This not only conserves resources but also reduces pollution and soil degradation, leading to more sustainable farming practices.
- **Organic Farming and Certification**: AI can support organic farming by monitoring compliance with organic standards and ensuring traceability from farm to fork. This is particularly relevant in India, where organic farming is gaining popularity but often faces challenges related to certification and market access.

5. Government Initiatives and Policy Support

- **Digital India and AI in Agriculture**: The Indian government has launched several initiatives under the Digital India program to promote the use of AI in agriculture. These initiatives include setting up AI research centers, promoting digital literacy among farmers, and encouraging the use of AI in various agricultural schemes.
- **Collaboration with Private Sector and Startups**: The Indian government is also fostering partnerships with private companies and startups to develop and deploy AI solutions for agriculture. This has led to the emergence of numerous agri-tech startups that are leveraging AI to solve specific challenges in Indian agriculture.
- **Policy Framework for AI in Agriculture**: The government is working on creating a conducive policy framework that encourages the adoption of AI in agriculture while ensuring data privacy, security, and inclusivity. This includes setting up regulatory guidelines and standards for AI applications in the agricultural sector.

6. Case Studies of AI Application in Indian Agriculture

- **Microsoft's AI for Earth**: Microsoft, in collaboration with the International Crop Research Institute for the Semi-Arid Tropics (ICRISAT), has developed an AI-based sowing app. This app uses AI to provide advisories on the optimal sowing time based on weather data, leading to increased yields for farmers in Andhra Pradesh.
- **IBM Watson Decision Platform**: IBM's AI-powered platform helps Indian farmers make data-driven decisions by analyzing weather data, soil conditions, and crop health. This platform has been used in several states to improve agricultural productivity and reduce risks.
- **NITI Aayog and AI in Agriculture**: NITI Aayog, in collaboration with various stakeholders, has been promoting AI-driven projects in agriculture. These projects include AI for soil health monitoring, pest control, and crop yield prediction, benefiting farmers across the country.

7. Future Prospects

- **Scaling AI Adoption**: While AI adoption in Indian agriculture is still in its early stages, the future holds immense potential. With increasing awareness, technological advancements, and supportive policies, AI could become a mainstream tool in Indian agriculture, transforming the sector.

- **Integration with Emerging Technologies**: The integration of AI with other emerging technologies such as the Internet of Things (IoT), blockchain, and robotics will further enhance its relevance in Indian agriculture. These combined technologies can provide a holistic solution to the challenges faced by Indian farmers.
- **Empowering Marginalized Farmers**: AI has the potential to democratize access to information and technology, empowering marginalized farmers in remote areas. With the right infrastructure and support, AI can help reduce the digital divide and ensure that all farmers benefit from technological advancements.

CHAPTER II

Current Scenario of Indian Agriculture

Overview of Indian Agriculture

Indian agriculture is a vital sector that plays a crucial role in the country's economy, livelihood, and cultural heritage. With a diverse range of agro-climatic zones, a vast agricultural landscape, and a significant proportion of the population engaged in farming, Indian agriculture is a cornerstone of national development.

1. Historical Context

- **Ancient and Colonial Periods**: Agriculture has been the backbone of India's economy for centuries. In ancient times, India was known for its advanced agricultural practices and was a major exporter of spices, cotton, and other crops. The Green Revolution in the 1960s marked a turning point, leading to self-sufficiency in food grains and transforming India from a food-deficit nation to a food-surplus one.
- **Post-Independence Era**: After gaining independence in 1947, India focused on agricultural development through land reforms, irrigation projects, and the establishment of agricultural universities. The introduction of high-yielding varieties (HYVs) of seeds, along with chemical fertilizers and pesticides during the Green Revolution, significantly boosted agricultural productivity.

2. Current Status of Indian Agriculture

- **Contribution to the Economy**: Agriculture contributes around 16-17% to India's Gross Domestic Product (GDP) and provides employment to nearly 50% of the workforce. It is the primary source of livelihood for millions of people, especially in rural areas.
- **Diverse Agro-Climatic Zones**: India is endowed with diverse agro-climatic conditions, ranging from tropical to temperate, which allows the cultivation of a wide variety of crops. The country is divided into 15 agro-climatic zones, each supporting different types of farming activities.

- **Major Crops**: India is one of the world's largest producers of several crops, including rice, wheat, sugarcane, cotton, and spices. The country is also a major producer of horticultural products like fruits, vegetables, and flowers, as well as plantation crops such as tea, coffee, and rubber.
- **Livestock and Dairy**: India has a significant livestock population, with dairy farming being a crucial component of the agricultural sector. India is the world's largest producer of milk, contributing to both domestic consumption and exports.

3. Agricultural Practices and Systems

- **Traditional Farming**: A large portion of Indian agriculture is still dependent on traditional farming methods, particularly among small and marginal farmers. These practices include crop rotation, intercropping, and mixed farming, which are often more sustainable but less productive compared to modern techniques.
- **Modernization and Mechanization**: In recent decades, there has been a gradual shift towards modern agricultural practices, including the use of mechanized equipment, advanced irrigation systems, and high-yielding seed varieties. However, the extent of modernization varies widely across regions, with some areas still lagging behind.
- **Organic Farming**: India is witnessing a growing trend towards organic farming, driven by increasing awareness of health and environmental issues. Organic farming is being promoted through government initiatives and the growing demand for organic products in domestic and international markets.
- **Sustainable Practices**: Sustainable agricultural practices, including integrated pest management (IPM), conservation tillage, and agroforestry, are gaining importance as concerns about environmental degradation and climate change grow.

4. Challenges in Indian Agriculture

- **Fragmented Landholdings**: The average landholding size in India is small, with a significant proportion of farmers owning less than two hectares of land. This fragmentation poses challenges for mechanization, efficient resource use, and achieving economies of scale.

- **Dependence on Monsoons**: Indian agriculture is highly dependent on monsoon rains, making it vulnerable to climate variability and water scarcity. Despite significant progress in irrigation, a large portion of farmland remains rain-fed, leading to fluctuations in agricultural output.
- **Low Productivity**: Compared to global standards, the productivity of many Indian crops remains low. This is due to factors such as poor soil health, inadequate access to quality inputs, and limited adoption of modern technologies.
- **Infrastructure Deficiencies**: Inadequate infrastructure, including poor rural roads, insufficient storage facilities, and a lack of cold chains, hampers the efficient movement of agricultural produce from farms to markets. This results in high post-harvest losses and reduced income for farmers.
- **Market Access and Pricing**: Farmers often face challenges in accessing markets and getting fair prices for their produce. The dominance of middlemen, limited access to market information, and volatility in prices exacerbate these issues, leading to distress among farmers.

5. Government Initiatives and Policies

- **Agricultural Reforms**: The Indian government has implemented various reforms aimed at improving the agricultural sector, including the promotion of contract farming, market reforms, and the introduction of digital platforms like e-NAM (National Agriculture Market) to connect farmers with buyers directly.
- **Subsidies and Support**: The government provides subsidies on inputs such as fertilizers, seeds, and electricity to support farmers. Minimum Support Prices (MSP) for certain crops ensure that farmers receive a guaranteed price, reducing their exposure to market fluctuations.
- **Irrigation and Water Management**: Programs like the Pradhan Mantri Krishi Sinchayee Yojana (PMKSY) aim to enhance irrigation coverage and promote efficient water use in agriculture. The focus is on creating infrastructure for water storage, distribution, and on-farm water management.
- **Crop Insurance**: The Pradhan Mantri Fasal Bima Yojana (PMFBY) is a flagship crop insurance scheme designed to protect farmers from the risks associated with crop failure due to natural calamities, pests, and diseases.

- **Research and Development**: India has a strong network of agricultural research institutions under the Indian Council of Agricultural Research (ICAR). These institutions focus on developing new crop varieties, improving farming practices, and addressing emerging challenges like climate change.

6. Future Prospects

- **Technology Adoption**: The future of Indian agriculture will likely be shaped by the adoption of new technologies, including precision farming, drones, AI, and IoT. These technologies can help address challenges related to productivity, resource use efficiency, and sustainability.
- **Agri-Tech Startups**: India is witnessing a surge in agri-tech startups that are leveraging technology to offer solutions across the agricultural value chain. These startups are providing innovative services in areas such as farm management, supply chain optimization, and market access.
- **Sustainability and Climate Resilience**: As climate change poses increasing risks to agriculture, there will be a greater focus on developing climate-resilient crops, promoting sustainable farming practices, and enhancing the resilience of agricultural systems.
- **Diversification and Value Addition**: Diversification into high-value crops, horticulture, dairy, and fisheries, along with value addition through food processing, is expected to play a crucial role in enhancing farmers' incomes and reducing dependency on traditional crops.

Challenges Faced by Indian Farmers

Indian farmers face numerous challenges that affect their productivity, income, and overall well-being. These challenges are multifaceted, encompassing economic, environmental, and social dimensions. Addressing these issues is crucial for improving agricultural sustainability and ensuring the livelihood security of millions of farmers across the country.

1. Fragmented Landholdings

- **Small and Fragmented Farms**: A significant portion of Indian farmers operate on small and fragmented landholdings. The average landholding size is less than two hectares, which limits the ability to adopt modern farming techniques and achieve economies of scale. Small landholdings also make it difficult for farmers to access credit, invest in technology, and implement efficient resource management practices.

2. Dependence on Monsoons

- **Rainfed Agriculture**: A large part of Indian agriculture is rain-dependent, making it highly vulnerable to the variability of monsoon rains. Erratic rainfall patterns, either in the form of droughts or floods, can severely affect crop yields and lead to financial distress for farmers. Although irrigation infrastructure has improved over the years, many regions still lack adequate irrigation facilities.
- **Water Scarcity**: Water scarcity, exacerbated by over-extraction of groundwater and inefficient irrigation practices, is a major concern. In many areas, groundwater levels have dropped to critical levels, threatening the sustainability of agriculture.

3. Low Agricultural Productivity

- **Yield Gaps**: Despite being one of the largest producers of various crops, India's agricultural productivity remains low compared to global standards. Factors contributing to low productivity include poor soil health, inadequate access to quality seeds, fertilizers, and pesticides, and limited use of modern farming practices.
- **Post-Harvest Losses**: Significant post-harvest losses due to inadequate storage facilities, poor transportation infrastructure, and lack of processing facilities further reduce the effective yield and income of farmers.

4. Financial Constraints

- **Limited Access to Credit**: Small and marginal farmers often struggle to access formal credit, relying instead on informal sources such as moneylenders, who charge exorbitant interest rates. This leads to a cycle of debt that many farmers find difficult to escape.
- **High Input Costs**: The rising cost of agricultural inputs such as seeds, fertilizers, pesticides, and machinery is a major burden for farmers. Without access to affordable credit, many farmers resort to borrowing at high-interest rates, which can lead to indebtedness.

5. Market Access and Price Volatility

- **Fluctuating Prices**: Farmers frequently face volatile prices for their produce due to fluctuations in supply and demand, lack of market access, and inadequate market information. This volatility often results in farmers not receiving fair compensation for their produce.
- **Middlemen Dominance**: The agricultural marketing system in India is often dominated by middlemen who take a significant share of the profits, leaving farmers with low returns. The absence of direct market access and insufficient infrastructure for storage and transportation exacerbates this issue.

6. Environmental and Climate Challenges

- **Climate Change**: Climate change poses a significant threat to Indian agriculture, with increasing instances of extreme weather events such as heatwaves, floods, and cyclones. These events can cause crop failures, reduce yields, and lead to economic losses.
- **Soil Degradation**: Intensive farming practices, overuse of chemical fertilizers, and poor soil management have led to soil degradation, affecting soil fertility and productivity. Soil erosion, salinization, and loss of organic matter are pressing concerns.

7. Lack of Infrastructure

- **Inadequate Storage Facilities**: The lack of adequate storage facilities, particularly for perishable goods, leads to significant post-harvest losses. Cold storage infrastructure is especially lacking, which affects the preservation of fruits, vegetables, and dairy products.
- **Poor Transportation**: Poor rural road networks and transportation infrastructure make it difficult for farmers to transport their produce to markets in a timely manner, resulting in delays and potential losses in quality.

8. Technological Gaps

- **Limited Mechanization**: Despite advancements in agricultural technology, many Indian farmers still rely on traditional farming methods. Limited access to modern machinery and tools reduces the efficiency of farm operations and increases the labor burden on farmers.

- **Digital Divide**: The adoption of digital tools and technologies in agriculture, such as mobile-based advisory services, precision farming, and e-commerce platforms, is hindered by the digital divide. Many farmers lack access to smartphones, reliable internet connectivity, and the necessary skills to use these technologies effectively.

9. Socio-Economic Challenges

- **Farmer Suicides**: The agrarian distress in India has led to a tragic rise in farmer suicides, driven by factors such as indebtedness, crop failures, and the inability to secure fair prices. The socio-economic pressures faced by farmers are immense and often compounded by the lack of adequate social safety nets.
- **Aging Farmer Population**: The farming population in India is aging, with younger generations increasingly moving to urban areas in search of better employment opportunities. This trend poses a challenge to the sustainability of agriculture as the older generation of farmers may lack the physical ability to manage farms effectively and may be less open to adopting new technologies.

10. Policy and Governance Issues

- **Policy Implementation Gaps**: While the Indian government has introduced several policies and schemes to support farmers, there are significant gaps in implementation. Issues such as delays in subsidy disbursements, lack of awareness among farmers about available schemes, and bureaucratic hurdles often undermine the effectiveness of these initiatives.
- **Inadequate Research and Extension Services**: Agricultural research and extension services in India are not always aligned with the needs of farmers, particularly smallholders. The dissemination of research findings and innovative practices is often slow and limited, hindering the adoption of new technologies and practices that could improve productivity and sustainability.

Traditional vs. Modern Agricultural Practices

Agriculture has evolved significantly over time, with traditional and modern practices offering different approaches to farming. Each has its advantages and challenges, and understanding these differences helps in appreciating how agricultural practices impact productivity, sustainability, and farmer livelihoods.

1. Traditional Agricultural Practices

Definition: Traditional agricultural practices are those developed and passed down through generations. They are typically based on local knowledge, customs, and environmental conditions.

Characteristics:

- **Labor-Intensive**: Traditional farming is often labor-intensive, relying on manual tools and techniques. Farmers use methods like hand plowing, planting, and harvesting.
- **Low Input**: Traditional practices generally use minimal synthetic inputs such as fertilizers, pesticides, and herbicides. Instead, organic methods like composting and natural pest control are common.
- **Crop Diversity**: Farmers grow a variety of crops in the same field, often incorporating intercropping and crop rotation to maintain soil fertility and reduce pest outbreaks.
- **Water Management**: Traditional irrigation methods include rainwater harvesting, small-scale irrigation channels, and manual watering, which may be less efficient compared to modern systems.
- **Knowledge-Based**: Practices are often based on local ecological knowledge and customs, adapted to the specific needs of the environment and crop varieties.

Advantages:

- **Sustainability**: Lower reliance on synthetic inputs and practices that maintain soil health contribute to long-term sustainability.
- **Biodiversity**: Diverse cropping systems support a range of plant and animal species, contributing to ecological balance.
- **Cultural Heritage**: Traditional methods are deeply rooted in cultural and community traditions, preserving local knowledge and practices.

Challenges:

- **Low Productivity**: Traditional methods often result in lower yields compared to modern practices due to limited access to high-yielding varieties and technologies.
- **Labor Intensity**: The reliance on manual labor can be physically demanding and may not be feasible for large-scale operations.
- **Limited Technology**: Traditional practices may lack the technological advancements needed to address modern challenges like climate change and resource scarcity.

2. Modern Agricultural Practices

Definition: Modern agricultural practices involve the use of advanced technologies, scientific research, and innovative techniques to enhance productivity, efficiency, and sustainability.

Characteristics:

- **Technology-Driven**: Modern farming utilizes machinery, precision agriculture, and technology such as GPS, drones, and automated systems for planting, harvesting, and monitoring crops.
- **High Input**: Modern practices often involve the use of synthetic fertilizers, pesticides, herbicides, and genetically modified organisms (GMOs) to increase crop yields and manage pests.
- **Monoculture**: Large-scale farms may practice monoculture, growing a single crop over large areas to maximize efficiency and simplify management.
- **Irrigation Systems**: Modern irrigation techniques, including drip and sprinkler systems, provide efficient water use and can be managed with automation.
- **Data and Analytics**: Modern agriculture relies on data collection and analysis for decision-making, including weather forecasting, soil health monitoring, and yield prediction.

Advantages:

- **Increased Productivity**: Advanced technologies and high-yielding varieties result in higher crop yields and improved efficiency.
- **Efficiency**: Mechanization and automation reduce the need for manual labor and increase operational efficiency.

- **Resource Management**: Precision agriculture techniques allow for more efficient use of resources such as water, fertilizers, and pesticides.

Challenges:

- **Environmental Impact**: The use of synthetic chemicals and monoculture can lead to soil degradation, loss of biodiversity, and water pollution.
- **High Costs**: Modern agricultural technologies and inputs can be expensive, creating barriers for small and marginal farmers.
- **Dependency**: Farmers may become dependent on technology and inputs from corporations, potentially leading to issues of sustainability and economic vulnerability.

3. Comparative Analysis

- **Productivity**: Modern practices generally offer higher productivity and efficiency compared to traditional methods, but this can come at the cost of environmental sustainability and high input requirements.
- **Sustainability**: Traditional practices are often more sustainable and environmentally friendly but may not meet the increasing food demands of a growing population. Modern practices, while efficient, may pose risks to environmental health if not managed properly.
- **Economic Viability**: Modern agriculture can be more economically viable for large-scale operations due to higher yields and efficiency. However, traditional practices often support smallholder farmers and local economies by preserving cultural practices and local knowledge.
- **Environmental Impact**: Traditional practices tend to have a lower environmental impact due to reduced chemical use and diverse cropping systems. Modern practices, while improving productivity, need to address the environmental challenges associated with high input use and monoculture.

4. Integration of Practices

Many experts advocate for an integrated approach that combines the strengths of both traditional and modern practices. This approach, often referred to as sustainable or conservation agriculture, aims to balance productivity with environmental stewardship and resource efficiency. Key elements of this integration include:

- **Agroecology**: Incorporating ecological principles into modern farming to enhance biodiversity and soil health while improving productivity.
- **Precision Agriculture**: Using technology to optimize resource use and minimize environmental impact, combined with traditional knowledge for local adaptation.
- **Organic Farming**: Applying organic farming principles within modern systems to reduce dependency on synthetic inputs and enhance soil fertility.
- **Climate-Smart Agriculture**: Adapting practices to cope with climate change while maintaining productivity and sustainability.

The Need for Technological Interventions in Agriculture

Technological interventions in agriculture are increasingly vital due to the sector's growing challenges and the need for improved productivity, sustainability, and efficiency. These interventions can address a range of issues, from resource management to market access, and are crucial for transforming agriculture to meet global food demands while ensuring environmental stewardship.

1. Addressing Resource Constraints

Water Management:

- **Irrigation Technologies**: Efficient irrigation systems like drip and sprinkler irrigation reduce water wastage and improve water use efficiency. Technologies such as soil moisture sensors and automated irrigation systems help in precise water management, essential in water-scarce regions.

Soil Health:

- **Precision Agriculture**: Technologies such as soil sensors and mapping tools provide detailed information about soil health, enabling targeted use of fertilizers and amendments. This reduces overuse of inputs and improves soil fertility.

Energy Efficiency:

- **Renewable Energy**: Solar-powered irrigation systems and wind-powered machinery can reduce dependency on fossil fuels and lower operational costs.

2. Enhancing Productivity
Crop Management:

- **Genetically Modified Crops**: GMOs can enhance crop resistance to pests, diseases, and environmental stresses, leading to higher yields and reduced losses.
- **Precision Farming**: Using GPS, drones, and satellite imagery for monitoring crop health, optimizing planting patterns, and managing nutrients. This technology enables farmers to make data-driven decisions, leading to increased productivity.

Automation:

- **Farm Machinery**: Modern machinery such as automated tractors, harvesters, and planters can increase efficiency and reduce the labor required for various farming operations.

Data Analytics:

- **Big Data**: Analyzing large datasets to predict weather patterns, track crop performance, and optimize planting schedules. Data-driven insights help in making informed decisions and improving overall farm management.

3. Improving Sustainability
Environmental Impact:

- **Sustainable Practices**: Technologies that promote sustainable farming practices, such as reduced tillage and cover cropping, help in conserving soil and water resources.
- **Waste Management**: Innovations in composting and biogas production from agricultural waste can reduce environmental impact and recycle nutrients back into the soil.

Climate Adaptation:

- **Climate-Smart Agriculture**: Implementing technologies that help farmers adapt to changing climatic conditions, such as drought-resistant crops and early warning systems for extreme weather events.

Biodiversity:

- **Integrated Pest Management (IPM)**: Technology-assisted IPM strategies reduce reliance on chemical pesticides and promote ecological balance.

4. Enhancing Market Access and Economic Viability
Market Information:

- **Mobile Apps and Platforms**: Digital platforms provide farmers with real-time market prices, weather forecasts, and agricultural advice. This information helps in making better marketing decisions and accessing fair prices.

E-Commerce:

- **Online Marketplaces**: Platforms that connect farmers directly with consumers or buyers reduce the dependency on middlemen, ensuring better prices for their produce.

Financial Services:

- **Digital Finance**: Mobile banking and digital financial services offer easier access to credit and insurance, which are crucial for managing risks and investing in farm improvements.

5. Overcoming Labor Shortages
Labor-saving Technologies:

- **Automation**: Robotics and automated systems for planting, weeding, and harvesting address labor shortages and increase efficiency.

- **Smart Farming**: Technologies like sensors and IoT devices can reduce the need for manual labor by automating monitoring and control processes.

6. Enhancing Knowledge and Skills
Training and Education:

- **E-Learning Platforms**: Online courses and tutorials provide farmers with access to the latest agricultural practices, technologies, and market trends.
- **Extension Services**: Digital extension services offer real-time advice and support, helping farmers implement new technologies and practices effectively.

7. Facilitating Research and Innovation
R&D:

- **Collaborative Platforms**: Technology facilitates collaboration between researchers, farmers, and industry stakeholders to develop and disseminate innovative solutions.
- **Field Trials**: Digital tools enable more efficient design, execution, and analysis of field trials, accelerating the development of new technologies and practices.

Technological interventions are essential for modernizing agriculture and addressing the sector's challenges. By improving resource management, enhancing productivity, promoting sustainability, and providing better market access, technology plays a crucial role in transforming agriculture. The adoption of these technologies can lead to more resilient and efficient farming systems, ultimately contributing to food security and sustainable development. However, it is important to ensure that technological advancements are accessible to all farmers, including smallholders, and that they are integrated with traditional knowledge and practices for optimal outcomes.

CHAPTER III

AI Technologies in Indian Agriculture

Machine Learning and Data Analytics in Agriculture

Machine learning (ML) and data analytics are revolutionizing agriculture by providing farmers and agricultural professionals with powerful tools to improve decision-making, optimize resources, and enhance productivity. These technologies leverage vast amounts of data to uncover insights, predict outcomes, and drive efficiencies across various aspects of farming.

1. Machine Learning in Agriculture

Definition: Machine learning is a subset of artificial intelligence (AI) that involves training algorithms to recognize patterns and make predictions based on data. In agriculture, ML algorithms analyze data from various sources to generate actionable insights and automate processes.

Applications:

- **Crop Health Monitoring**: ML algorithms analyze satellite imagery and drone data to detect signs of plant diseases, pests, or nutrient deficiencies. This early detection allows for timely intervention and reduces crop losses.
- **Yield Prediction**: ML models predict crop yields based on historical data, weather patterns, soil conditions, and crop management practices. Accurate yield forecasts help in planning and optimizing resource allocation.
- **Precision Agriculture**: ML analyzes data from soil sensors, weather stations, and drones to provide recommendations on precise amounts of water, fertilizers, and pesticides. This approach enhances resource efficiency and minimizes environmental impact.
- **Automated Harvesting**: ML-powered robots and machinery can identify ripe crops and automate harvesting tasks, reducing labor costs and improving harvesting efficiency.
- **Supply Chain Optimization**: ML algorithms optimize supply chain operations by predicting demand, managing inventory, and improving logistics. This reduces waste and ensures timely delivery of produce to markets.

Advantages:

- **Enhanced Decision-Making**: ML provides actionable insights that help farmers make data-driven decisions, improving efficiency and productivity.
- **Early Detection**: ML algorithms can detect issues such as pest infestations or disease outbreaks before they become widespread, enabling prompt intervention.
- **Resource Optimization**: ML helps in optimizing the use of resources such as water, fertilizers, and pesticides, leading to cost savings and environmental benefits.

Challenges:

- **Data Quality and Availability**: Effective ML models require high-quality, comprehensive data. Inconsistent or incomplete data can impact the accuracy of predictions.
- **Technical Expertise**: Implementing ML solutions requires specialized knowledge and skills, which may be a barrier for some farmers.
- **Cost**: The initial investment in ML technologies and infrastructure can be high, particularly for smallholders.

2. Data Analytics in Agriculture

Definition: Data analytics involves examining and interpreting large datasets to extract meaningful insights and inform decision-making. In agriculture, data analytics encompasses a range of techniques to analyze data from various sources, including sensors, satellite imagery, and historical records.

Applications:

- **Precision Farming**: Data analytics helps in understanding soil health, weather patterns, and crop conditions. By analyzing this data, farmers can make precise decisions about planting, irrigation, and fertilization.
- **Climate Adaptation**: Analyzing climate data helps farmers adapt to changing weather patterns and develop strategies for managing risks related to climate change.
- **Farm Management**: Data analytics tools assist in managing farm operations, including planning, budgeting, and tracking performance.

They provide insights into operational efficiencies and cost savings.

- **Market Analysis:** Data analytics helps in understanding market trends, consumer preferences, and price fluctuations. This information enables farmers to make informed marketing decisions and negotiate better prices.
- **Supply Chain Management:** Analytics optimize supply chain processes by analyzing data on inventory, demand, and logistics, leading to more efficient distribution and reduced waste.

Advantages:

- **Improved Efficiency:** Data analytics provides insights that help in optimizing farm operations, reducing waste, and improving overall efficiency.
- **Informed Decision-Making:** By analyzing data, farmers can make better decisions regarding crop management, resource allocation, and risk management.
- **Enhanced Predictive Capabilities:** Analytics tools can forecast trends and outcomes, helping farmers prepare for potential challenges and opportunities.

Challenges:

- **Data Integration:** Combining data from various sources (e.g., sensors, satellites, and historical records) can be complex and requires effective integration systems.
- **Data Security:** Protecting sensitive agricultural data from breaches and unauthorized access is crucial.
- **Data Literacy:** Farmers need to develop data literacy skills to effectively interpret and use analytics results.

3. Integration of ML and Data Analytics
Complementary Roles:

- **Data-Driven Insights:** ML and data analytics complement each other by providing data-driven insights that can be used to train ML models. For example, historical weather data analyzed through data analytics can be used to improve ML models for yield prediction.

- **Real-Time Monitoring**: Combining ML with data analytics allows for real-time monitoring of crop health and environmental conditions, enabling timely responses and adjustments.

Practical Examples:

- **Smart Farming Platforms**: Integrated platforms combine ML algorithms with data analytics to provide comprehensive solutions for crop management, resource optimization, and supply chain management.
- **Decision Support Systems**: These systems use ML and data analytics to offer recommendations and forecasts, assisting farmers in making informed decisions based on real-time data.

Machine learning and data analytics are transforming agriculture by enhancing productivity, optimizing resource use, and improving decision-making. While there are challenges in implementing these technologies, their potential benefits in terms of efficiency, sustainability, and profitability make them essential tools for the future of agriculture. As technology continues to advance, the integration of ML and data analytics will play a crucial role in addressing the complex challenges faced by the agricultural sector and driving innovation in farming practices.

AI-Driven Precision Farming

AI-driven precision farming represents a transformative approach to agriculture, leveraging advanced technologies to optimize crop production, resource use, and farm management. By integrating artificial intelligence (AI) with precision farming techniques, this approach aims to enhance productivity, sustainability, and efficiency in modern agriculture.

1. Concept of Precision Farming

Definition: Precision farming, also known as precision agriculture, is an approach that uses technology to monitor and manage field variability in crops. The goal is to optimize field-level management regarding crop farming. AI enhances precision farming by providing data-driven insights and automating various processes.

Key Components:

- **Data Collection**: Utilizes sensors, drones, satellites, and other technologies to gather data on soil conditions, crop health, weather, and other variables.

- **Data Analysis**: Involves processing and analyzing the collected data to make informed decisions. AI algorithms play a crucial role in this step, offering predictive analytics and actionable insights.
- **Variable Rate Technology**: Implements adjustments in real-time to the application of inputs like water, fertilizers, and pesticides based on data-driven recommendations.

2. Applications of AI in Precision Farming
Crop Monitoring:

- **Disease and Pest Detection**: AI-powered image recognition systems analyze images from drones or cameras to identify signs of diseases or pests. Early detection allows for targeted treatment, reducing crop losses.
- **Growth Monitoring**: AI algorithms analyze data from sensors and satellite imagery to assess crop growth patterns and identify areas needing attention.

Soil Management:

- **Soil Health Monitoring**: AI analyzes data from soil sensors to monitor moisture levels, nutrient content, and pH levels. This information helps in optimizing soil management practices.
- **Nutrient Management**: AI models predict nutrient requirements and recommend precise fertilizer application rates, reducing excess use and improving crop yields.

Water Management:

- **Irrigation Optimization**: AI systems use data from weather forecasts, soil moisture sensors, and crop water requirements to automate and optimize irrigation schedules, reducing water wastage.
- **Drought Prediction**: AI analyzes climate data to predict drought conditions, enabling proactive water management strategies.

Yield Prediction:

- **Forecasting**: AI algorithms analyze historical data, weather patterns, and current crop conditions to predict yield outcomes. Accurate predictions help in planning and market strategy.

- **Harvest Timing**: AI tools determine the optimal time for harvesting based on crop maturity and weather conditions, improving yield quality and reducing losses.

Automation and Robotics:

- **Autonomous Vehicles**: AI-driven robots and autonomous tractors perform tasks such as planting, weeding, and harvesting with high precision, reducing the need for manual labor.
- **Smart Machinery**: AI-powered machinery adjusts operations in real-time based on data inputs, such as adjusting seeding depth or applying the right amount of fertilizer.

3. Benefits of AI-Driven Precision Farming
Increased Efficiency:

- **Optimized Resource Use**: AI ensures precise application of resources like water, fertilizers, and pesticides, leading to cost savings and reduced environmental impact.
- **Labor Reduction**: Automation and AI-driven machinery decrease the need for manual labor, improving operational efficiency.

Enhanced Productivity:

- **Higher Yields**: AI-driven insights and precise management practices result in improved crop yields and quality.
- **Predictive Maintenance**: AI helps in maintaining machinery and equipment by predicting failures and scheduling maintenance, reducing downtime.

Sustainability:

- **Environmental Protection**: AI-driven precision farming minimizes the overuse of chemicals and water, contributing to sustainable agricultural practices.
- **Reduced Waste**: By optimizing input use and improving yield predictions, AI reduces agricultural waste and enhances resource

efficiency.

Improved Decision-Making:

- **Data-Driven Insights**: AI provides actionable insights and recommendations based on real-time data, enabling better decision-making and planning.
- **Risk Management**: AI helps in identifying and managing risks related to weather, pests, and diseases, improving resilience and adaptability.

4. Challenges and Considerations
Data Privacy and Security:

- **Data Protection**: Safeguarding sensitive agricultural data from breaches and unauthorized access is essential.
- **Compliance**: Adhering to regulations and standards related to data privacy and security is crucial for protecting farmers' information.

Cost and Accessibility:

- **Investment**: The initial cost of AI technologies and infrastructure can be high, particularly for smallholder farmers.
- **Technology Access**: Ensuring equitable access to AI technologies and training is important for widespread adoption and benefits.

Integration with Existing Practices:

- **Adaptation**: Integrating AI-driven precision farming with traditional practices requires careful planning and adaptation to local conditions.
- **Training**: Providing training and support to farmers to effectively use AI technologies is necessary for successful implementation.

5. Future Prospects
Advancements:

- **Enhanced Algorithms**: Continued advancements in AI algorithms and models will improve accuracy, efficiency, and scalability in precision farming.

- **Integration with IoT**: The integration of AI with Internet of Things (IoT) devices will enable more comprehensive and real-time monitoring of agricultural processes.

Global Adoption:

- **Widespread Use**: As technology becomes more affordable and accessible, AI-driven precision farming is expected to see wider adoption across different regions and farming scales.
- **Sustainable Agriculture**: AI will play a key role in promoting sustainable agriculture practices by optimizing resource use and reducing environmental impact.

AI-driven precision farming represents a significant advancement in agricultural technology, offering numerous benefits in terms of efficiency, productivity, and sustainability. By leveraging AI to analyze data and automate processes, farmers can optimize resource use, improve crop yields, and enhance overall farm management. Despite challenges related to cost, accessibility, and integration, the future of AI in precision farming looks promising, with continued advancements expected to drive innovation and address global agricultural challenges.

Internet of Things (IoT) and Smart Sensors in Agriculture

The Internet of Things (IoT) and smart sensors are transforming agriculture by enabling real-time monitoring, data collection, and automation. These technologies facilitate precise management of agricultural practices, leading to improved efficiency, productivity, and sustainability.

1. Concept of IoT and Smart Sensors

Internet of Things (IoT):

- **Definition**: IoT refers to the network of interconnected devices and systems that communicate and exchange data over the internet. In agriculture, IoT integrates various sensors, machines, and devices to create a connected ecosystem that provides actionable insights and automation.
- **Components**: IoT systems typically include sensors, communication networks, data processing units, and user interfaces. These components work together to collect, transmit, analyze, and present data.

Smart Sensors:

- **Definition**: Smart sensors are devices equipped with the capability to measure physical parameters (e.g., temperature, humidity, soil moisture) and process data locally or transmit it to other systems for analysis.
- **Functions**: Smart sensors collect real-time data, perform initial data processing, and provide insights that can be used for decision-making or automated actions.

2. Applications of IoT and Smart Sensors in Agriculture
Soil Monitoring:

- **Soil Moisture Sensors**: Measure the moisture content in the soil, allowing for precise irrigation management. Data helps in optimizing water usage and preventing over- or under-watering.
- **Soil Nutrient Sensors**: Monitor soil nutrient levels, providing information on the need for fertilizers and soil amendments. This ensures balanced nutrient supply for optimal crop growth.

Crop Health Management:

- **Climate Sensors**: Monitor environmental conditions such as temperature, humidity, and light levels. Data helps in understanding crop health and detecting potential stress factors.
- **Disease and Pest Detection**: Sensors combined with image recognition systems detect symptoms of plant diseases and pest infestations, enabling early intervention and targeted treatment.

Irrigation Management:

- **Automated Irrigation Systems**: IoT-enabled irrigation systems use soil moisture data and weather forecasts to automate and optimize irrigation schedules. This reduces water wastage and ensures efficient use of resources.
- **Weather Stations**: Collect data on weather conditions to forecast and plan irrigation needs, pest management, and other agricultural activities.

Farm Equipment and Machinery:

- **Precision Agriculture Machinery**: IoT-connected tractors and harvesters monitor performance and conditions in real-time. Data from these machines helps in optimizing their operations and scheduling maintenance.
- **Automation**: Smart sensors and IoT devices enable automated planting, weeding, and harvesting, reducing the need for manual labor and improving efficiency.

Livestock Management:

- **Wearable Sensors**: Monitor the health and activity levels of livestock. Data on temperature, movement, and behavior helps in managing animal health and productivity.
- **Feeding Systems**: IoT-enabled feeding systems optimize feed distribution based on individual animal needs, improving growth rates and feed efficiency.

Supply Chain Management:

- **Tracking and Monitoring**: IoT devices track the location and condition of agricultural products during transport, ensuring quality and reducing spoilage.
- **Inventory Management**: IoT systems monitor stock levels and manage inventory, optimizing storage and reducing waste.

3. Benefits of IoT and Smart Sensors in Agriculture
Enhanced Efficiency:

- **Optimized Resource Use**: Real-time data allows for precise management of water, nutrients, and inputs, leading to cost savings and reduced environmental impact.
- **Automated Operations**: Automation of various farming tasks reduces manual labor, improves accuracy, and increases operational efficiency.

Improved Productivity:

- **Better Crop Yields**: Accurate monitoring and management of crop and soil conditions lead to healthier plants and higher yields.

- **Efficient Livestock Management**: Monitoring livestock health and activity enhances productivity and reduces losses.

Sustainability:

- **Resource Conservation**: Efficient use of water and nutrients minimizes waste and supports sustainable farming practices.
- **Reduced Environmental Impact**: IoT systems help in minimizing the use of harmful chemicals and reducing the carbon footprint of agricultural operations.

Real-Time Insights:

- **Data-Driven Decisions**: Access to real-time data enables farmers to make informed decisions and respond promptly to changes in conditions.
- **Early Problem Detection**: Early detection of issues such as diseases, pests, or equipment failures allows for timely intervention and reduces potential damage.

4. Challenges and Considerations
Data Privacy and Security:

- **Data Protection**: Ensuring the security of data collected by IoT devices is crucial to protect sensitive information and prevent unauthorized access.
- **Compliance**: Adhering to regulations and standards related to data privacy and security is important for maintaining trust and protecting user information.

Cost and Accessibility:

- **Initial Investment**: The cost of IoT devices, sensors, and infrastructure can be high, particularly for small-scale farmers.
- **Technology Access**: Ensuring equitable access to IoT technologies and providing training for their effective use are important for widespread adoption.

Integration and Interoperability:

- **System Integration**: Integrating various IoT devices and systems into a cohesive ecosystem requires careful planning and technical expertise.
- **Standardization**: Lack of standardization among IoT devices and platforms can lead to compatibility issues and hinder seamless operation.

Data Management:

- **Data Overload**: Managing and analyzing large volumes of data generated by IoT devices can be challenging. Effective data processing and analysis tools are necessary.

5. Future Prospects
Advancements:

- **Improved Sensors**: Continued advancements in sensor technology will lead to more accurate and affordable devices for various agricultural applications.
- **AI Integration**: Combining IoT with artificial intelligence will enhance data analysis capabilities, leading to more sophisticated insights and automation.

Global Adoption:

- **Widespread Use**: As technology becomes more accessible and affordable, IoT and smart sensors are expected to see broader adoption across different regions and farming scales.
- **Sustainable Practices**: IoT will play a key role in promoting sustainable agriculture by optimizing resource use and reducing environmental impact.

IoT and smart sensors are revolutionizing agriculture by providing real-time monitoring, data collection, and automation capabilities. These technologies enhance efficiency, productivity, and sustainability in farming practices. While there are challenges related to cost, data security, and system integration, the benefits of IoT and smart sensors make them essential tools for modern agriculture. Continued advancements and wider adoption of these technologies will drive innovation and address global agricultural challenges, paving the way for more resilient and sustainable farming systems.

Robotics and Automation in Farming

Robotics and automation are increasingly becoming integral parts of modern agriculture, revolutionizing how farming tasks are performed. By incorporating robots and automated systems into agricultural practices, farmers can achieve higher efficiency, productivity, and precision. This shift towards automation addresses many traditional farming challenges and opens new avenues for innovation in agriculture.

1. Overview of Robotics and Automation in Agriculture

Robotics in Agriculture:

- **Definition**: Robotics in agriculture refers to the use of robots to perform various tasks related to crop production, soil management, and livestock care. These robots can operate autonomously or be remotely controlled, providing a range of functions from planting to harvesting.
- **Types of Agricultural Robots:**

  - **Autonomous Tractors**: Self-driving tractors equipped with GPS and sensors for plowing, planting, and tilling.
  - **Harvesting Robots**: Robots designed to pick fruits and vegetables with precision, minimizing damage to crops.
  - **Weeding Robots**: Robots that identify and remove weeds using mechanical, thermal, or chemical methods.
  - **Planting Robots**: Robots that automate the process of planting seeds at precise depths and intervals.

Automation in Agriculture:

- **Definition**: Automation in agriculture involves using technology to perform repetitive or complex tasks without human intervention. This includes the use of machinery, control systems, and software to streamline farming processes.
- **Components of Agricultural Automation:**

  - **Automated Machinery**: Equipment such as combines, planters, and sprayers that operate with minimal human input.

- ○ **Control Systems**: Software and sensors that manage and monitor agricultural operations, adjusting parameters in real-time.
- ○ **Data Integration**: Systems that integrate data from various sources (e.g., sensors, drones) to optimize farming practices.

2. Applications of Robotics and Automation in Farming
Crop Management:

- **Planting and Seeding**: Automated planting systems ensure accurate seed placement, depth, and spacing, which enhances crop growth and yields.
- **Harvesting**: Harvesting robots equipped with advanced sensors and AI identify ripe crops and pick them with minimal damage, improving efficiency and reducing labor costs.
- **Weeding and Pest Control**: Robotics and automation systems target weeds and pests with precision, using mechanical or chemical methods to reduce competition for resources and control pests.

Soil and Water Management:

- **Soil Preparation**: Automated tractors and tillers prepare the soil for planting by plowing, harrowing, and leveling with precision.
- **Irrigation**: Automated irrigation systems use data from soil moisture sensors and weather forecasts to optimize water usage, reducing waste and ensuring adequate watering.

Livestock Management:

- **Feeding Systems**: Automated feeders distribute feed according to individual animal needs, improving feed efficiency and reducing labor.
- **Health Monitoring**: Robotics and sensors track the health and behavior of livestock, detecting early signs of illness and optimizing care.

Farm Monitoring and Management:

- **Drones**: Drones equipped with cameras and sensors monitor crop health, soil conditions, and field performance, providing valuable data for decision-making.

- **Autonomous Vehicles**: Vehicles such as robots and drones navigate fields to perform tasks like scouting, mapping, and data collection.

3. Benefits of Robotics and Automation in Agriculture
Increased Efficiency:

- **Labor Reduction**: Automation reduces the need for manual labor, allowing farmers to focus on more strategic tasks and manage larger areas more efficiently.
- **Precision**: Robots and automated systems perform tasks with high precision, optimizing input use (e.g., fertilizers, pesticides) and reducing waste.

Enhanced Productivity:

- **Higher Yields**: Accurate planting, harvesting, and crop management increase overall crop yields and quality.
- **Timely Operations**: Automated systems operate around the clock, ensuring timely completion of tasks such as planting and harvesting.

Cost Savings:

- **Reduced Labor Costs**: Automation decreases labor costs associated with manual farming tasks.
- **Optimized Resource Use**: Precise application of resources (e.g., water, fertilizers) reduces input costs and minimizes environmental impact.

Improved Sustainability:

- **Resource Conservation**: Automation helps in conserving resources by optimizing their use and reducing waste.
- **Reduced Environmental Impact**: Automated systems minimize the use of chemicals and reduce soil compaction and erosion.

Enhanced Data Collection and Analysis:

- **Real-Time Monitoring**: Robots and sensors collect real-time data on crop and soil conditions, enabling informed decision-making and timely interventions.

- **Predictive Analytics**: Data collected by automated systems can be analyzed to predict trends, manage risks, and improve farm management practices.

4. Challenges and Considerations
Cost of Implementation:

- **Initial Investment**: The upfront cost of robotic systems and automated machinery can be high, posing a barrier for small and medium-sized farms.
- **Maintenance and Repairs**: Maintaining and repairing sophisticated robotic systems requires specialized knowledge and resources.

Technical Skills and Training:

- **Skill Requirements**: Operating and maintaining robotic systems and automated machinery require technical skills and training.
- **Training Programs**: Providing training and support to farmers for effective use of new technologies is essential for successful adoption.

Integration with Existing Practices:

- **Compatibility**: Integrating new robotic systems with existing farming practices and equipment can be challenging and may require adjustments.
- **Adaptation**: Farmers may need to adapt their practices and workflows to fully leverage the benefits of automation.

Data Privacy and Security:

- **Data Management**: Ensuring the security and privacy of data collected by robotic systems is crucial to protect sensitive information.
- **Cybersecurity**: Implementing robust cybersecurity measures to safeguard against data breaches and unauthorized access is important.

5. Future Prospects
Advancements:

- **Improved Robotics**: Advances in robotics will lead to more versatile and affordable machines capable of performing a wider range of tasks.
- **AI Integration**: Combining robotics with AI will enhance the capabilities of agricultural robots, enabling more sophisticated decision-making and automation.

Wider Adoption:

- **Scalability**: As technology becomes more accessible and affordable, the adoption of robotics and automation is expected to increase across various farm sizes and regions.
- **Sustainable Agriculture**: Robotics and automation will play a key role in promoting sustainable agricultural practices by optimizing resource use and reducing environmental impact.

Innovation:

- **New Applications**: Continued research and development will lead to new applications and innovations in robotics and automation, addressing emerging agricultural challenges.

Robotics and automation are transforming agriculture by enhancing efficiency, productivity, and sustainability. By reducing labor requirements, optimizing resource use, and improving precision, these technologies offer significant benefits for modern farming. Despite challenges related to cost, technical skills, and integration, the future of robotics and automation in agriculture looks promising, with continued advancements expected to drive innovation and address global agricultural needs.

AI-Based Weather Forecasting and Predictive Analytics in Agriculture

AI-based weather forecasting and predictive analytics are revolutionizing agriculture by providing farmers with accurate and timely weather information, enabling better decision-making and risk management. By leveraging artificial intelligence (AI) and machine learning (ML) algorithms, these technologies enhance the ability to predict weather patterns and assess their impact on agricultural activities.

1. AI in Weather Forecasting

Definition:

- **AI-Based Weather Forecasting**: AI-based weather forecasting utilizes machine learning algorithms and data analytics to predict weather conditions more accurately than traditional methods. It involves analyzing vast amounts of historical and real-time weather data to identify patterns and make predictions.

Key Components:

- **Data Collection**: AI systems gather data from various sources, including satellites, weather stations, radar, and sensors. This data includes temperature, humidity, wind speed, precipitation, and atmospheric pressure.
- **Machine Learning Models**: Algorithms such as neural networks, decision trees, and ensemble methods analyze historical weather data and identify complex patterns to predict future weather conditions.
- **Integration**: AI models integrate data from multiple sources, including weather satellites and ground-based sensors, to generate comprehensive forecasts.

Advantages:

- **Improved Accuracy**: AI models can analyze complex datasets and account for various factors influencing weather patterns, leading to more accurate forecasts.
- **Real-Time Updates**: AI-based systems provide real-time weather updates, allowing farmers to receive timely information about changing weather conditions.
- **Localized Forecasts**: AI enables highly localized forecasts, providing weather information specific to a particular region or even a specific farm.

2. Predictive Analytics in Agriculture
Definition:

- **Predictive Analytics**: Predictive analytics involves using statistical techniques and machine learning algorithms to analyze historical and real-time data to predict future events and trends. In agriculture, it helps forecast various aspects such as crop yields, pest infestations, and disease outbreaks.

Applications:

- **Crop Yield Prediction**: AI models analyze factors such as weather conditions, soil health, crop type, and historical yield data to predict future crop yields. This helps farmers plan their production and optimize resource allocation.
- **Pest and Disease Forecasting**: Predictive analytics models use weather data, crop health information, and historical pest and disease occurrence to forecast potential outbreaks. This allows farmers to implement preventive measures and reduce the impact on their crops.
- **Irrigation Management**: AI-based predictive models analyze weather forecasts and soil moisture data to optimize irrigation schedules. This helps in conserving water and ensuring crops receive adequate moisture.
- **Fertilizer and Pesticide Application**: Predictive analytics helps determine the optimal timing and amount of fertilizer and pesticide application based on weather conditions, crop growth stages, and historical data.

3. Benefits of AI-Based Weather Forecasting and Predictive Analytics Enhanced Decision-Making:

- **Timely Information**: Accurate weather forecasts and predictive analytics provide farmers with timely information to make informed decisions about planting, harvesting, and managing crops.
- **Risk Management**: Predictive analytics helps farmers anticipate potential risks such as extreme weather events, pest infestations, and disease outbreaks, enabling proactive measures to mitigate damage.

Increased Productivity:

- **Optimized Resource Use**: AI-based systems help optimize the use of resources such as water, fertilizers, and pesticides by providing precise recommendations based on predictive models.
- **Improved Planning**: Accurate forecasts and predictions allow farmers to plan their activities more effectively, leading to better crop management and increased yields.

Cost Savings:

- **Reduced Losses**: By anticipating and mitigating risks, farmers can reduce losses related to weather-related damage, pest infestations, and diseases.
- **Efficient Resource Allocation**: Predictive analytics helps allocate resources more efficiently, reducing waste and lowering costs associated with inputs and labor.

Sustainability:

- **Environmental Protection**: Optimized use of resources and targeted interventions reduce the environmental impact of agricultural practices, promoting sustainability.
- **Climate Adaptation**: AI-based forecasting and predictive analytics support adaptation to changing climate conditions by providing insights into long-term trends and patterns.

4. Challenges and Considerations
Data Quality and Availability:

- **Data Accuracy**: The accuracy of AI-based predictions depends on the quality and completeness of the data used. Incomplete or inaccurate data can lead to less reliable forecasts.
- **Data Integration**: Integrating data from various sources and ensuring its consistency can be challenging, particularly in regions with limited data infrastructure.

Complexity of Models:

- **Algorithm Complexity**: AI and ML models can be complex and require specialized knowledge to develop, implement, and interpret.
- **Model Training**: Training AI models requires extensive historical data and computational resources, which may not be available in all regions.

Cost and Accessibility:

- **Implementation Costs**: The initial cost of implementing AI-based forecasting and predictive analytics systems can be high, particularly for small-scale farmers.
- **Technology Access**: Ensuring equitable access to advanced technologies and providing training for their effective use is essential for widespread adoption.

Privacy and Security:

- **Data Privacy**: Protecting the privacy of data collected and used by AI systems is crucial to prevent unauthorized access and misuse.
- **Cybersecurity**: Implementing robust cybersecurity measures to safeguard data and systems from potential threats is important.

5. Future Prospects
Advancements:

- **Improved Algorithms**: Ongoing advancements in AI and ML algorithms will enhance the accuracy and reliability of weather forecasting and predictive analytics.
- **Integration with IoT**: Combining AI with IoT technologies will enable more comprehensive and real-time data collection, leading to better predictions and recommendations.

Global Adoption:

- **Wider Reach**: As technology becomes more accessible and affordable, AI-based forecasting and predictive analytics are expected to see broader adoption across different regions and farming scales.
- **Enhanced Support**: Increased support and investment in data infrastructure and training will drive the adoption and effectiveness of AI-based systems.

Innovation:

- **New Applications**: Continued research and development will lead to innovative applications of AI in agriculture, addressing emerging challenges and opportunities.

AI-based weather forecasting and predictive analytics are transforming agriculture by providing accurate, real-time information and insights. These technologies enhance decision-making, improve productivity, and promote sustainability. While challenges related to data quality, model complexity, and cost remain, the future prospects for AI in agriculture are promising, with continued advancements expected to drive innovation and address global agricultural needs.

Drones and Satellite Imaging in Agriculture

Drones and satellite imaging are cutting-edge technologies that are significantly enhancing agricultural practices. By providing high-resolution imagery and data, these technologies enable farmers to monitor crop health, manage resources efficiently, and make informed decisions. The integration of drones and satellite imaging into agriculture offers numerous benefits and opens new possibilities for precision farming.

1. Drones in Agriculture

Definition:

- **Drones**: Unmanned aerial vehicles (UAVs) equipped with cameras, sensors, and GPS systems used for aerial surveillance and data collection in agriculture.

Key Components:

- **Multispectral and RGB Cameras**: Drones are equipped with multispectral sensors that capture data beyond visible light, providing information on plant health and soil conditions. RGB cameras capture high-resolution images for visual analysis.
- **GPS and IMU**: Drones use GPS for precise navigation and positioning, while Inertial Measurement Units (IMUs) ensure stable flight and accurate data capture.
- **Data Transmission and Processing**: Drones transmit data in real-time or store it for later processing. Data is analyzed using software to generate maps and reports.

Applications:

- **Crop Monitoring**: Drones provide real-time aerial imagery of crops, allowing farmers to monitor plant health, growth patterns, and detect issues such as nutrient deficiencies, diseases, and pests.

- **Field Mapping**: Drones create detailed maps of fields, including plant density, soil health, and topography. This information helps in planning and managing agricultural practices.
- **Precision Agriculture**: Drones facilitate precision agriculture by providing data for site-specific management of resources such as water, fertilizers, and pesticides.
- **Irrigation Management**: Drones equipped with thermal imaging sensors can identify areas of water stress in crops, helping optimize irrigation practices.

Benefits:

- **Enhanced Monitoring**: Drones offer high-resolution, real-time data that improves the accuracy of crop monitoring and management.
- **Efficiency**: Drones can cover large areas quickly and efficiently, reducing the time and labor required for field inspections.
- **Cost Savings**: By identifying issues early and optimizing resource use, drones can help reduce input costs and improve crop yields.

Challenges:

- **Regulations**: Compliance with aviation regulations and obtaining necessary permits can be challenging, particularly in densely populated or restricted areas.
- **Data Management**: Processing and analyzing large volumes of data collected by drones requires specialized software and expertise.
- **Initial Cost**: The upfront cost of purchasing and maintaining drones can be high, which may be a barrier for small-scale farmers.

2. Satellite Imaging in Agriculture
Definition:

- **Satellite Imaging**: The use of satellite technology to capture images and data of the Earth's surface. Satellites provide broad-scale observations and can monitor agricultural areas over time.

Key Components:

- **Optical and Radar Sensors**: Satellites use optical sensors for visible and near-infrared imaging and radar sensors for capturing information in various weather conditions.
- **Data Resolution**: Satellites offer different levels of resolution, from coarse to high-resolution imagery, depending on the application.
- **Data Integration**: Satellite data is integrated with other sources of information (e.g., ground-based measurements) for comprehensive analysis.

Applications:

- **Crop Health Monitoring**: Satellite imagery helps monitor crop health, growth stages, and identify stress factors such as drought, pests, and diseases.
- **Yield Estimation**: Satellite data is used to estimate crop yields by analyzing vegetation indices and growth patterns.
- **Land Use and Management**: Satellites provide data on land use changes, crop rotation, and land cover, aiding in land management and planning.
- **Disaster Management**: Satellite imagery assists in assessing the impact of natural disasters (e.g., floods, droughts) on agriculture and planning recovery efforts.

Benefits:

- **Broad Coverage**: Satellites offer extensive coverage and can monitor large agricultural areas, providing a comprehensive view of farming practices.
- **Long-Term Monitoring**: Satellite data provides historical records, enabling the analysis of long-term trends and changes in agricultural practices.
- **Cost-Effective**: Once in orbit, satellites can continuously provide data without the need for physical access to the fields, reducing monitoring costs.

Challenges:

- **Resolution Limitations**: Some satellites may offer lower resolution images that are less suitable for detailed analysis.

- **Data Latency**: There may be a delay in receiving and processing satellite data, which can affect real-time decision-making.
- **Cost of High-Resolution Imagery**: High-resolution satellite imagery can be expensive, which may limit access for some farmers.

3. Integration of Drones and Satellite Imaging
Synergy:

- **Complementary Data**: Combining drone and satellite data provides a comprehensive view of agricultural operations. Drones offer high-resolution, localized data, while satellites provide broad-scale observations and long-term monitoring.
- **Enhanced Analysis**: Integrating data from both sources allows for more accurate analysis and decision-making, including improved crop monitoring, yield estimation, and resource management.
- **Optimized Resource Use**: The combined insights from drones and satellites enable precise and targeted interventions, optimizing the use of water, fertilizers, and pesticides.

Applications:

- **Precision Farming**: The integration of drone and satellite data supports precision farming by providing detailed and accurate information for site-specific management.
- **Agricultural Research**: Researchers use combined data to study crop growth patterns, soil conditions, and environmental impacts, leading to advancements in agricultural practices.
- **Disaster Response**: In the event of natural disasters, combined imagery helps assess damage and plan recovery efforts more effectively.

4. Future Prospects
Technological Advancements:

- **Improved Sensors**: Advances in sensor technology will enhance the capabilities of both drones and satellites, providing more detailed and accurate data.
- **AI Integration**: Integrating AI with drone and satellite data will improve data analysis, automate decision-making, and offer predictive insights.

Wider Adoption:

- **Increased Accessibility**: As technology becomes more affordable and accessible, more farmers will adopt drones and satellite imaging for agricultural management.
- **Enhanced Collaboration**: Collaboration between technology providers, researchers, and farmers will drive innovation and support the development of practical solutions.

Innovation:

- **New Applications**: Ongoing research and development will lead to new applications of drone and satellite technology in agriculture, addressing emerging challenges and opportunities.

Drones and satellite imaging are transforming agriculture by providing valuable insights and data for crop monitoring, resource management, and decision-making. The integration of these technologies enhances precision farming, improves productivity, and promotes sustainability. While challenges related to cost, data management, and resolution exist, advancements in technology and wider adoption are expected to drive further innovation and benefits in the agricultural sector.

Blockchain and AI for Supply Chain Management in Agriculture

Blockchain and Artificial Intelligence (AI) are revolutionizing supply chain management in agriculture by improving transparency, efficiency, and traceability. These technologies address various challenges in the agricultural supply chain, from production to consumer delivery, and offer innovative solutions for optimizing operations.

1. Blockchain in Supply Chain Management
Definition:

- **Blockchain**: A decentralized digital ledger technology that records transactions across multiple computers in a secure, transparent, and immutable manner. Each transaction, or "block," is linked to the previous one, forming a chain of records.

Key Components:

- **Distributed Ledger**: A shared database maintained by multiple participants, ensuring transparency and reducing the risk of fraud.
- **Smart Contracts**: Self-executing contracts with the terms of the agreement directly written into code, automating and enforcing contract execution.
- **Consensus Mechanisms**: Protocols used to validate transactions and maintain the integrity of the blockchain, such as Proof of Work (PoW) or Proof of Stake (PoS).

Applications in Agriculture:

- **Traceability**: Blockchain provides a transparent and immutable record of every transaction and movement of agricultural products from farm to table. This enhances traceability, allowing consumers to verify the origin and quality of products.
- **Food Safety**: By tracking the entire supply chain, blockchain helps quickly identify and address issues related to food safety, such as contamination or recalls. This improves response times and reduces the impact of foodborne illnesses.
- **Fraud Prevention**: Blockchain's transparency and immutability help prevent fraud by ensuring that records cannot be altered or tampered with, protecting against issues like mislabeling or counterfeit products.
- **Supply Chain Optimization**: Blockchain enables real-time tracking and verification of products, improving inventory management, reducing waste, and optimizing logistics.

Benefits:

- **Increased Transparency**: Provides a clear and accessible record of transactions and movements, enhancing trust among stakeholders.
- **Enhanced Security**: Immutable records and decentralized control reduce the risk of data manipulation and fraud.
- **Improved Efficiency**: Automation through smart contracts and streamlined processes reduce administrative overhead and delays.

Challenges:

- **Integration**: Integrating blockchain with existing supply chain systems can be complex and may require significant changes to current practices.
- **Scalability**: Handling large volumes of transactions and data on a blockchain can be challenging, particularly for global supply chains.
- **Adoption**: Widespread adoption requires collaboration and agreement among various stakeholders, which can be difficult to achieve.

2. AI in Supply Chain Management
Definition:

- **Artificial Intelligence (AI)**: The simulation of human intelligence processes by machines, particularly computer systems. AI includes machine learning, natural language processing, and other technologies that enable computers to perform tasks that typically require human intelligence.

Key Components:

- **Machine Learning (ML)**: Algorithms that analyze data to identify patterns and make predictions. ML models are used for demand forecasting, inventory management, and optimizing supply chain processes.
- **Natural Language Processing (NLP)**: AI technology that enables computers to understand and interpret human language, useful for processing textual data and customer interactions.
- **Robotic Process Automation (RPA)**: AI-driven automation of repetitive tasks, such as data entry and order processing, to improve efficiency and accuracy.

Applications in Agriculture:

- **Demand Forecasting**: AI algorithms analyze historical sales data, market trends, and external factors (e.g., weather) to predict future demand, helping farmers and suppliers plan production and inventory levels more accurately.
- **Inventory Management**: AI optimizes inventory levels by predicting demand and adjusting supply accordingly. This reduces excess inventory and minimizes shortages.

- **Supply Chain Optimization**: AI analyzes data from various sources to optimize logistics, such as route planning, transportation scheduling, and warehouse management. This improves efficiency and reduces costs.
- **Predictive Maintenance**: AI monitors equipment and machinery to predict and prevent breakdowns, ensuring smooth operations and reducing downtime.

Benefits:

- **Enhanced Decision-Making**: AI provides actionable insights and predictions based on data analysis, supporting better decision-making in supply chain management.
- **Improved Efficiency**: Automation and optimization of processes reduce operational costs, streamline workflows, and enhance overall efficiency.
- **Increased Accuracy**: AI reduces human error by providing accurate forecasts, inventory levels, and operational recommendations.

Challenges:

- **Data Quality**: AI models rely on high-quality data for accurate predictions and insights. Poor or incomplete data can lead to unreliable results.
- **Implementation Costs**: Developing and implementing AI solutions can be expensive and may require significant investment in technology and expertise.
- **Integration**: Integrating AI with existing supply chain systems and processes can be complex and may require adjustments to current practices.

**3. Integration of Blockchain and AI in Supply Chain Management
Synergy:**

- **Enhanced Transparency and Efficiency**: Combining blockchain's transparency with AI's predictive capabilities provides a more efficient and reliable supply chain. Blockchain ensures secure and transparent record-keeping, while AI optimizes processes and forecasts.
- **Data Integration**: AI can analyze data stored on the blockchain, providing insights and recommendations for improving supply chain

operations. This integration supports more informed decision-making.

- **Automated Smart Contracts**: AI can automate the execution of smart contracts on the blockchain, streamlining processes such as payments, order fulfillment, and compliance.

Applications:

- **End-to-End Visibility**: The integration of blockchain and AI provides comprehensive visibility across the entire supply chain, from production to delivery. This enables better coordination and responsiveness.
- **Fraud Detection and Prevention**: AI algorithms can analyze blockchain data to detect and prevent fraudulent activities, ensuring the integrity of the supply chain.
- **Supply Chain Resilience**: Combining blockchain's transparency with AI's predictive analytics enhances the resilience of the supply chain by enabling proactive risk management and response.

Benefits:

- **Comprehensive Insight**: The integration offers a holistic view of the supply chain, improving transparency, efficiency, and risk management.
- **Increased Trust**: Enhanced data integrity and visibility build trust among stakeholders, including consumers, suppliers, and regulators.
- **Optimized Operations**: AI-driven insights and blockchain's secure record-keeping optimize supply chain operations, reducing costs and improving performance.

Challenges:

- **Complexity**: Integrating blockchain and AI can be complex and may require significant changes to existing systems and processes.
- **Data Privacy**: Ensuring data privacy and security while integrating AI and blockchain is essential to protect sensitive information.
- **Adoption Barriers**: Widespread adoption of integrated blockchain and AI solutions may face resistance due to cost, complexity, and the need for collaboration among stakeholders.

Blockchain and AI are transforming supply chain management in agriculture by enhancing transparency, efficiency, and traceability. Blockchain provides a secure and transparent record of transactions, while AI offers predictive analytics and automation to optimize operations. The integration of these technologies provides a comprehensive approach to managing the agricultural supply chain, addressing challenges and improving overall performance. While there are challenges related to implementation and integration, the benefits of combining blockchain and AI offer significant opportunities for innovation and advancement in agricultural supply chain management.

CHAPTER IV

Applications of AI in Indian Agriculture

Crop Monitoring and Disease Detection

Crop monitoring and disease detection are crucial components of modern agriculture, aiming to optimize crop health, improve yields, and minimize losses. Advanced technologies, including AI, remote sensing, and IoT, play a pivotal role in enhancing these processes. Here's an overview of how these technologies are used for crop monitoring and disease detection:

1. Traditional Methods of Crop Monitoring and Disease Detection
Visual Inspection:

- **Manual Checks**: Farmers and agronomists traditionally inspect crops manually for signs of disease, pest damage, and other issues. This method is labor-intensive and time-consuming.
- **Field Surveys**: Regular field surveys involve inspecting random samples of crops to assess their health and detect potential problems.

Limitations:

- **Labor-Intensive**: Manual inspections require significant time and effort, particularly in large fields.
- **Subjective**: Human observations can be inconsistent and may miss subtle symptoms or early-stage problems.
- **Delayed Detection**: Issues may not be identified until they have progressed, leading to reduced effectiveness of treatments.

2. Remote Sensing Technologies
Definition:

- **Remote Sensing**: The use of satellite or aerial imagery to collect data about crops without direct contact. This technology provides a broad perspective on crop health and environmental conditions.

Key Components:

- **Satellites**: Provide global and regional-scale imagery. Satellites can capture data on vegetation indices, temperature, and moisture levels.
- **Drones**: Offer high-resolution, localized imagery. Drones can be equipped with multispectral and thermal sensors to monitor crop health and detect anomalies.

Applications:

- **Vegetation Indices**: Remote sensing data is used to calculate indices such as the Normalized Difference Vegetation Index (NDVI), which indicates plant health and stress levels.
- **Disease Detection**: Changes in vegetation indices and thermal imaging can reveal early signs of diseases and pest infestations.
- **Moisture and Temperature Monitoring**: Remote sensing helps monitor soil moisture and crop temperature, which are critical for assessing crop health and irrigation needs.

Benefits:

- **Broad Coverage**: Provides a comprehensive view of large areas quickly and efficiently.
- **Early Detection**: Identifies issues before they become widespread, allowing for timely interventions.
- **Data Integration**: Combines with other data sources for more accurate analysis.

Challenges:

- **Cost**: High-resolution imagery and remote sensing equipment can be expensive.
- **Data Processing**: Analyzing and interpreting large volumes of data requires specialized software and expertise.

3. AI and Machine Learning in Crop Monitoring and Disease Detection

Definition:

- **Artificial Intelligence (AI)**: The simulation of human intelligence processes by machines. AI can analyze complex data patterns and make predictions.
- **Machine Learning (ML)**: A subset of AI that involves training algorithms to recognize patterns and make predictions based on data.

Key Components:

- **Image Recognition**: AI algorithms analyze images from drones, satellites, or cameras to detect symptoms of diseases, pests, and nutrient deficiencies.
- **Predictive Analytics**: Machine learning models use historical data to predict disease outbreaks and pest invasions based on environmental conditions and crop health.
- **Data Integration**: AI integrates data from various sources (e.g., remote sensing, weather data) to provide comprehensive insights.

Applications:

- **Disease Diagnosis**: AI-powered image recognition systems can identify disease symptoms on leaves and stems, providing accurate diagnoses and treatment recommendations.
- **Pest Detection**: Machine learning models analyze patterns in imagery to detect pest infestations and assess their severity.
- **Growth Monitoring**: AI monitors crop growth stages and health, providing insights into optimal harvest times and resource needs.

Benefits:

- **Enhanced Accuracy**: AI improves the accuracy of disease and pest detection by analyzing detailed data and patterns.
- **Timely Interventions**: Predictive analytics allow for proactive measures, reducing the impact of diseases and pests.
- **Scalability**: AI solutions can scale to handle large volumes of data from multiple sources.

Challenges:

- **Data Quality**: AI models require high-quality, labeled data for accurate predictions and analysis.
- **Complexity**: Developing and training AI models can be complex and may require specialized knowledge.
- **Integration**: Integrating AI solutions with existing agricultural practices and systems can be challenging.

4. IoT and Smart Sensors in Crop Monitoring
Definition:

- **Internet of Things (IoT)**: A network of interconnected devices that collect and exchange data. In agriculture, IoT devices include sensors and smart systems that monitor environmental conditions and crop health.

Key Components:

- **Soil Sensors**: Measure soil moisture, temperature, pH, and nutrient levels to provide insights into soil health and irrigation needs.
- **Weather Stations**: Collect data on temperature, humidity, rainfall, and other weather parameters that affect crop health.
- **Plant Health Sensors**: Monitor plant physiological parameters, such as leaf temperature and chlorophyll levels, to assess crop health.

Applications:

- **Real-Time Monitoring**: IoT sensors provide real-time data on soil and environmental conditions, allowing for immediate adjustments to irrigation, fertilization, and pest control.
- **Automated Irrigation**: Smart irrigation systems use sensor data to optimize water usage based on crop needs and soil moisture levels.
- **Condition Monitoring**: IoT devices track and report on crop and soil conditions, helping to identify potential problems early.

Benefits:

- **Data-Driven Decisions**: IoT provides detailed, real-time data that supports informed decision-making.

- **Resource Efficiency**: Optimizes resource use, reducing waste and improving productivity.
- **Automation**: Automates routine tasks, such as irrigation, reducing labor and increasing efficiency.

Challenges:

- **Cost**: Initial setup and maintenance of IoT systems can be expensive.
- **Data Management**: Managing and analyzing large volumes of data from multiple sensors requires robust systems and expertise.
- **Connectivity**: Reliable internet connectivity is essential for IoT systems, which can be a challenge in remote areas.

Advanced technologies such as remote sensing, AI, and IoT are transforming crop monitoring and disease detection by providing accurate, real-time data and insights. Remote sensing offers broad-scale observations, while AI enhances disease and pest detection through advanced data analysis. IoT and smart sensors provide continuous monitoring of environmental and crop conditions, enabling timely and precise interventions. These technologies collectively improve crop health management, optimize resource use, and enhance productivity, paving the way for more efficient and sustainable agricultural practices. However, challenges related to cost, data management, and integration must be addressed to fully realize their potential.

Soil Health Monitoring and Management

Soil health is fundamental to agricultural productivity and sustainability. Effective soil health monitoring and management involve assessing and maintaining soil conditions to optimize crop growth, enhance yields, and ensure environmental sustainability. Advances in technology, including IoT, AI, and remote sensing, play a crucial role in improving soil health management practices.

1. Importance of Soil Health

Definition:

- **Soil Health**: The capacity of soil to function as a living system that sustains plant and animal life, maintains or improves water and air quality, and supports ecosystem processes.

Key Factors:

- **Soil Structure**: The arrangement of soil particles into aggregates that affect water infiltration, root growth, and aeration.
- **Soil Fertility**: The presence of essential nutrients and organic matter necessary for plant growth.
- **Soil Moisture**: The amount of water available in the soil for plant uptake.
- **Soil pH**: The acidity or alkalinity of the soil, which affects nutrient availability and microbial activity.
- **Biological Activity**: The presence and activity of soil organisms that contribute to nutrient cycling and organic matter decomposition.

Benefits:

- **Enhanced Crop Yields**: Healthy soils provide optimal conditions for plant growth, leading to increased productivity.
- **Sustainable Agriculture**: Maintaining soil health supports long-term agricultural sustainability and reduces the need for chemical inputs.
- **Environmental Protection**: Healthy soils contribute to water filtration, carbon sequestration, and reduced erosion.

2. Traditional Methods of Soil Health Monitoring
Soil Testing:

- **Laboratory Analysis**: Soil samples are collected and analyzed in a laboratory to determine nutrient levels, pH, organic matter content, and other properties.
- **Interpretation**: Results are used to guide fertilization, liming, and other soil management practices.

Visual Inspection:

- **Field Observation**: Farmers inspect soil conditions visually, noting signs of erosion, compaction, or poor plant growth.

Limitations:

- **Labor-Intensive**: Soil testing and visual inspections require significant time and effort.
- **Snapshot in Time**: Traditional methods provide information based on specific samples and may not capture variations within the field.

3. Modern Technologies for Soil Health Monitoring
Internet of Things (IoT) and Smart Sensors:
Definition:

- **IoT**: A network of interconnected devices that collect and exchange data. In soil health monitoring, IoT devices include sensors that measure various soil parameters.

Key Components:

- **Soil Sensors**: Measure soil moisture, temperature, pH, and nutrient levels in real-time.
- **Weather Stations**: Collect data on weather conditions that affect soil health, such as rainfall and temperature.

Applications:

- **Real-Time Data Collection**: IoT sensors provide continuous monitoring of soil conditions, allowing for timely adjustments in irrigation and fertilization.
- **Automated Systems**: Smart irrigation systems use sensor data to optimize water usage based on soil moisture levels.

Benefits:

- **Continuous Monitoring**: Provides real-time data, enabling proactive management of soil health.
- **Resource Efficiency**: Optimizes resource use, such as water and fertilizers, based on real-time soil conditions.

Challenges:

- **Cost**: Initial setup and maintenance of IoT systems can be expensive.

- **Data Management**: Requires robust systems for managing and analyzing large volumes of data.

AI and Machine Learning:
Definition:

- **AI**: The simulation of human intelligence processes by machines, including machine learning, which involves training algorithms to recognize patterns and make predictions.

Key Components:

- **Data Analysis**: AI algorithms analyze soil data to identify patterns and predict soil health trends.
- **Predictive Modeling**: Machine learning models forecast soil conditions and recommend management practices based on historical data and environmental factors.

Applications:

- **Predictive Analytics**: AI models predict soil nutrient needs, potential issues, and optimal management practices.
- **Decision Support**: Provides actionable insights for soil management, improving decision-making processes.

Benefits:

- **Enhanced Accuracy**: AI improves the accuracy of soil health assessments and predictions.
- **Informed Decision-Making**: Offers data-driven recommendations for soil management.

Challenges:

- **Data Quality**: Requires high-quality, accurate data for effective modeling and predictions.
- **Complexity**: Developing and implementing AI models can be complex and require specialized knowledge.

Remote Sensing:
Definition:

- **Remote Sensing**: The use of satellite or aerial imagery to collect data about soil conditions without direct contact.

Key Components:

- **Satellite Imagery**: Provides large-scale observations of soil properties and land use.
- **Drones**: Offer high-resolution, localized imagery for detailed soil analysis.

Applications:

- **Soil Mapping**: Remote sensing data is used to create soil maps that show variations in soil properties across a field.
- **Erosion and Degradation Monitoring**: Detects signs of soil erosion, degradation, and other issues that affect soil health.

Benefits:

- **Broad Coverage**: Provides extensive coverage and detailed information over large areas.
- **Early Detection**: Identifies soil issues before they become severe, allowing for timely interventions.

Challenges:

- **Cost**: High-resolution imagery and remote sensing equipment can be expensive.
- **Data Processing**: Analyzing and interpreting remote sensing data requires specialized software and expertise.

4. Integrated Soil Health Management
Definition:

- **Integrated Soil Health Management**: A holistic approach that combines various technologies and practices to monitor and manage soil health effectively.

Components:

- **Combining Technologies**: Integrates IoT sensors, AI, and remote sensing to provide comprehensive soil health data and insights.
- **Sustainable Practices**: Implements practices such as cover cropping, reduced tillage, and organic amendments to maintain and improve soil health.

Applications:

- **Precision Agriculture**: Uses integrated data to optimize soil management practices, including irrigation, fertilization, and crop rotation.
- **Soil Conservation**: Implements conservation practices based on real-time data and predictive analytics to prevent erosion and degradation.

Benefits:

- **Comprehensive Management**: Provides a complete view of soil health, supporting more effective and sustainable management practices.
- **Enhanced Productivity**: Optimizes soil conditions to improve crop yields and overall farm productivity.

Challenges:

- **Complexity**: Integrating multiple technologies and practices requires careful planning and management.
- **Knowledge and Skills**: Effective implementation requires knowledge of soil science and technology.

Soil health monitoring and management are critical for sustainable agriculture and optimal crop production. Advances in technology, including IoT, AI, and remote sensing, provide powerful tools for monitoring soil conditions, predicting trends, and managing soil health effectively. While these technologies offer significant benefits, including real-time data, enhanced accuracy, and improved resource efficiency, they also come with challenges related to cost, data management, and integration. A holistic approach that combines these technologies with sustainable soil management practices can help ensure long-term soil health and agricultural productivity.

Irrigation Management and Water Resource Optimization

Effective irrigation management and water resource optimization are essential for sustainable agriculture, especially in regions facing water scarcity. Advances in technology, including AI, IoT, and precision agriculture tools, are transforming how water resources are managed and utilized in farming. Here's an in-depth look at these practices and technologies:

1. Importance of Irrigation Management

Definition:

- **Irrigation Management**: The process of planning, controlling, and optimizing the supply of water to crops to ensure their healthy growth while conserving water resources.

Key Objectives:

- **Maximize Crop Yields**: Ensure that crops receive adequate water to achieve optimal growth and yield.
- **Conserve Water**: Use water resources efficiently to minimize waste and reduce the environmental impact.
- **Maintain Soil Health**: Prevent waterlogging and salinization, which can adversely affect soil health and crop productivity.

Benefits:

- **Increased Productivity**: Proper irrigation management enhances crop yields and overall farm productivity.
- **Sustainable Water Use**: Optimizes water use, reducing wastage and ensuring long-term availability of water resources.
- **Improved Crop Health**: Provides consistent moisture levels, reducing stress and improving plant health.

2. Traditional Irrigation Methods
Surface Irrigation:

- **Flood Irrigation**: Water is applied to fields and allowed to flow over the surface by gravity. This method is simple but can lead to water wastage and uneven distribution.
- **Furrow Irrigation**: Water is directed into furrows or channels between crop rows. This method is more efficient than flood irrigation but still prone to water loss through evaporation and infiltration.

Drip Irrigation:

- **Definition**: Delivers water directly to the plant root zone through a network of pipes, valves, and emitters.
- **Advantages**: Reduces water wastage, minimizes evaporation, and ensures precise water application.

Sprinkler Irrigation:

- **Definition**: Water is sprayed over the crops through a system of pipes and sprinklers, simulating natural rainfall.
- **Advantages**: Provides uniform coverage and is suitable for a variety of crops and field sizes.

Limitations:

- **Water Loss**: Traditional methods can result in significant water loss due to evaporation, runoff, and deep percolation.
- **Inefficiency**: Surface irrigation methods may lead to uneven water distribution and inefficient use of water resources.

3. Modern Technologies for Irrigation Management
Internet of Things (IoT) and Smart Sensors:
Definition:

- **IoT**: A network of interconnected devices that collect and exchange data. In irrigation, IoT devices include sensors that monitor soil moisture, weather conditions, and crop water needs.

Key Components:

- **Soil Moisture Sensors**: Measure the moisture content in the soil, providing data on when and how much to irrigate.
- **Weather Sensors**: Collect data on rainfall, temperature, and humidity to help predict irrigation needs.
- **Flow Meters**: Monitor the amount of water applied through irrigation systems.

Applications:

- **Automated Irrigation**: IoT systems can automate irrigation based on real-time soil moisture data and weather forecasts.
- **Water Usage Monitoring**: Track and optimize water usage to reduce waste and improve efficiency.

Benefits:

- **Precision**: Provides accurate and timely data for precise irrigation decisions.
- **Resource Efficiency**: Optimizes water use, reducing waste and improving overall efficiency.

Challenges:

- **Cost**: Initial setup and maintenance of IoT systems can be expensive.
- **Data Management**: Requires robust systems for managing and analyzing data from multiple sensors.

AI and Machine Learning:
Definition:

- **AI**: The simulation of human intelligence processes by machines, including machine learning, which involves training algorithms to recognize patterns and make predictions.

Key Components:

- **Predictive Analytics**: AI models analyze historical data and current conditions to predict future irrigation needs and optimize water use.
- **Decision Support Systems**: AI provides actionable insights and recommendations for irrigation scheduling and water management.

Applications:

- **Demand Forecasting**: Predicts water requirements based on crop growth stages, weather conditions, and soil moisture levels.
- **Optimization**: AI algorithms optimize irrigation schedules and water distribution for maximum efficiency.

Benefits:

- **Enhanced Accuracy**: Improves the accuracy of irrigation decisions by analyzing complex data patterns.
- **Proactive Management**: Allows for proactive adjustments to irrigation practices based on predictive insights.

Challenges:

- **Data Quality**: Requires high-quality data for effective modeling and predictions.
- **Complexity**: Developing and implementing AI models can be complex and require specialized knowledge.

Precision Irrigation Techniques:
Definition:

- **Precision Irrigation**: Uses advanced technologies and data to apply water more accurately and efficiently to meet crop needs.

Key Techniques:

- **Variable Rate Irrigation (VRI)**: Adjusts the amount of water applied based on variations in soil conditions and crop requirements.
- **Soil Moisture-Based Scheduling**: Uses soil moisture data to determine optimal irrigation timing and amount.

Applications:

- **Site-Specific Management**: Tailors irrigation practices to specific areas within a field, addressing variations in soil and crop needs.
- **Water Saving**: Reduces water use by applying only the amount needed in different areas of the field.

Benefits:

- **Water Efficiency**: Maximizes water use efficiency, reducing waste and conserving resources.
- **Improved Yields**: Ensures crops receive adequate water for optimal growth and yield.

Challenges:

- **Implementation**: Requires investment in technology and infrastructure for effective implementation.
- **Data Integration**: Needs integration of various data sources for accurate decision-making.

Water Resource Optimization
Definition:

- **Water Resource Optimization**: The process of managing and utilizing water resources efficiently to meet agricultural needs while preserving resources for other uses.

Key Strategies:

- **Rainwater Harvesting**: Collecting and storing rainwater for irrigation and other uses.
- **Water Recycling**: Reusing water from irrigation and other sources for agricultural purposes.
- **Integrated Water Management**: Coordinating water use across different sectors (agriculture, industry, domestic) to ensure sustainable management.

Applications:

- **Water Management Plans**: Developing plans that outline water use, conservation measures, and efficiency goals.
- **Monitoring and Reporting**: Tracking water use and availability to inform management decisions and policies.

Benefits:

- **Sustainability**: Supports long-term sustainability of water resources and agricultural practices.
- **Resource Conservation**: Reduces water wastage and ensures availability for future needs.

Challenges:

- **Coordination**: Requires coordination among various stakeholders and sectors.
- **Infrastructure**: Investment in infrastructure and technology is needed for effective implementation.

Irrigation management and water resource optimization are critical for sustainable agriculture, particularly in water-scarce regions. Modern technologies, including IoT, AI, and precision irrigation techniques, offer powerful tools for improving irrigation practices, enhancing water use efficiency, and maximizing crop productivity. While these technologies provide significant benefits, such as precision, resource efficiency, and improved yields, they also come with challenges related to cost, data management, and implementation. A holistic approach that integrates advanced technologies with effective water management practices can help ensure the sustainable use of water resources and support agricultural productivity.

Yield Prediction and Forecasting

Yield prediction and forecasting are essential for effective agricultural management and planning. Accurate predictions help farmers, policymakers, and stakeholders make informed decisions about resource allocation, market strategies, and risk management. Advances in technology, including AI, machine learning, and remote sensing, are significantly enhancing the accuracy and reliability of yield predictions.

1. Importance of Yield Prediction and Forecasting

Definition:

- **Yield Prediction**: The process of estimating the quantity of crop production expected from a specific area based on various factors.
- **Yield Forecasting**: Involves predicting future crop yields using historical data, current conditions, and predictive models.

Key Objectives:

- **Resource Planning**: Helps in planning the allocation of resources such as fertilizers, water, and labor.
- **Market Preparation**: Assists in market forecasting and setting prices based on expected supply levels.
- **Risk Management**: Provides insights into potential risks and helps in developing strategies to mitigate them.

Benefits:

- **Optimized Resource Use**: Enables better management of inputs and resources based on expected yields.
- **Improved Decision-Making**: Supports strategic planning and decision-making for farmers and stakeholders.
- **Economic Stability**: Helps stabilize market prices and reduce economic uncertainties for farmers.

2. Traditional Methods of Yield Prediction

Historical Data Analysis:

- **Historical Yields**: Analyzing past yield data to predict future yields based on trends and patterns.
- **Field Observations**: Using visual inspection and manual measurements to estimate crop growth and potential yield.

Statistical Models:

- **Regression Analysis**: Applying statistical methods to correlate yield with various factors such as weather conditions, soil properties, and crop management practices.

Limitations:

- **Data Dependency**: Relies on historical data, which may not always account for current conditions or future changes.
- **Subjectivity**: Manual methods can be subjective and prone to errors.

3. Modern Technologies for Yield Prediction and Forecasting
Remote Sensing and Satellite Imagery:
Definition:

- **Remote Sensing**: The use of satellite or aerial imagery to collect data about crops and field conditions from a distance.

Key Components:

- **Satellite Imagery**: Provides large-scale observations of crop health, growth stages, and field conditions.
- **Drones**: Offer high-resolution, localized imagery for detailed analysis.

Applications:

- **Vegetation Indices**: Use indices such as NDVI (Normalized Difference Vegetation Index) to assess crop health and predict yields.
- **Growth Monitoring**: Tracks crop development and estimates yields based on growth patterns and conditions.

Benefits:

- **Broad Coverage**: Provides extensive data over large areas, improving the accuracy of predictions.
- **Real-Time Data**: Offers up-to-date information on crop conditions and potential yields.

Challenges:

- **Cost**: High-resolution imagery and remote sensing equipment can be expensive.
- **Data Processing**: Requires specialized software and expertise to analyze and interpret data.

AI and Machine Learning:
Definition:

- **AI**: Artificial Intelligence involves the simulation of human intelligence processes by machines, including machine learning for pattern recognition and prediction.

Key Components:

- **Predictive Models**: AI algorithms analyze historical and current data to predict future crop yields.
- **Pattern Recognition**: Machine learning models recognize patterns in data related to crop growth, weather, and soil conditions.

Applications:

- **Yield Forecasting Models**: AI models predict yields based on a combination of historical data, real-time observations, and environmental factors.
- **Decision Support**: Provides actionable insights and recommendations for optimizing crop management practices.

Benefits:

- **Enhanced Accuracy**: Improves the accuracy of yield predictions by analyzing complex data patterns.
- **Adaptability**: AI models can adapt to changing conditions and provide updated forecasts.

Challenges:

- **Data Quality**: Requires high-quality data for effective modeling and predictions.

- **Complexity**: Developing and implementing AI models can be complex and require specialized knowledge.

IoT and Smart Sensors:
Definition:

- **IoT**: A network of interconnected devices that collect and exchange data. In yield prediction, IoT devices include sensors that monitor soil conditions, weather, and crop health.

Key Components:

- **Soil Moisture Sensors**: Measure soil moisture levels, which influence crop growth and yield.
- **Weather Sensors**: Collect data on weather conditions that impact crop development.
- **Crop Health Sensors**: Monitor plant health and growth, providing data for yield predictions.

Applications:

- **Real-Time Monitoring**: Provides continuous data on crop and soil conditions for more accurate yield predictions.
- **Automated Systems**: Integrates data from various sensors to improve prediction models.

Benefits:

- **Precision**: Offers accurate and timely data for yield predictions.
- **Resource Efficiency**: Optimizes resource use based on real-time data.

Challenges:

- **Cost**: Initial setup and maintenance of IoT systems can be expensive.
- **Data Integration**: Requires integration of data from multiple sensors for accurate predictions.

Data Analytics and Big Data:

Definition:

- **Data Analytics**: The process of examining large datasets to uncover patterns, correlations, and insights. Big data involves managing and analyzing vast amounts of information.

Key Components:

- **Data Collection**: Gathering data from various sources, including sensors, satellite imagery, and historical records.
- **Data Analysis**: Using statistical and machine learning techniques to analyze data and predict yields.

Applications:

- **Predictive Analytics**: Analyzes historical and real-time data to forecast crop yields.
- **Trend Analysis**: Identifies trends and patterns that influence yield predictions.

Benefits:

- **Comprehensive Insights**: Provides a holistic view of factors affecting crop yields.
- **Improved Predictions**: Enhances the accuracy of yield forecasts by analyzing large volumes of data.

Challenges:

- **Data Management**: Requires robust systems for managing and processing large datasets.
- **Expertise**: Analyzing big data requires specialized knowledge and skills.

4. Integrated Approach to Yield Prediction
Definition:

- **Integrated Yield Prediction**: Combines various technologies and methods to provide a comprehensive approach to forecasting crop yields.

Components:

- **Combining Data Sources**: Integrates data from remote sensing, IoT sensors, AI models, and historical records.
- **Holistic Models**: Uses a combination of predictive models and real-time data to improve accuracy.

Applications:

- **Precision Agriculture**: Uses integrated data to optimize crop management and improve yield predictions.
- **Risk Management**: Provides insights into potential risks and helps develop strategies to mitigate them.

Benefits:

- **Enhanced Accuracy**: Improves yield predictions by combining multiple data sources and technologies.
- **Informed Decision-Making**: Supports better planning and decision-making for farmers and stakeholders.

Challenges:

- **Complexity**: Integrating multiple technologies and data sources can be complex and require careful management.
- **Cost**: Implementing an integrated approach may involve significant investment in technology and infrastructure.

Yield prediction and forecasting are crucial for optimizing agricultural productivity and resource management. Modern technologies, including remote sensing, AI, IoT, and big data analytics, are revolutionizing how yields are predicted, providing more accurate and timely insights. While these technologies offer significant benefits, such as enhanced accuracy and resource efficiency, they also present challenges related to cost, data management, and integration. Adopting an integrated approach that combines various technologies and methods can help improve yield predictions, support better decision-making, and contribute to sustainable agricultural practices.

Livestock Management and Health Monitoring

Effective livestock management and health monitoring are critical for ensuring the productivity, welfare, and overall health of livestock. Advances in technology, particularly AI, IoT, and data analytics, are transforming these practices, offering new solutions for monitoring and managing livestock more efficiently and proactively.

1. Importance of Livestock Management and Health Monitoring
Definition:

- **Livestock Management**: The process of overseeing and optimizing the care, breeding, and productivity of livestock to ensure their well-being and maximize agricultural output.
- **Health Monitoring**: The ongoing assessment of livestock health to detect and address any issues promptly, ensuring their overall well-being and productivity.

Key Objectives:

- **Optimize Productivity**: Improve growth rates, milk yield, and reproductive efficiency.
- **Ensure Animal Welfare**: Maintain high standards of care to promote the health and comfort of livestock.
- **Prevent Diseases**: Early detection and management of diseases to reduce losses and improve animal health.

Benefits:

- **Increased Efficiency**: Enhances the efficiency of livestock production and management practices.
- **Improved Health**: Reduces the incidence of diseases and health issues through proactive monitoring.
- **Economic Gains**: Increases profitability through improved productivity and reduced losses.

2. Traditional Livestock Management Practices
Manual Monitoring:

- **Visual Inspections**: Regular checks of livestock for signs of illness, injury, or poor condition.
- **Record Keeping**: Manual recording of health data, breeding information, and productivity metrics.

Husbandry Practices:

- **Feeding**: Traditional feeding practices based on available knowledge and resources.
- **Housing**: Basic housing and shelter to protect livestock from environmental elements.

Limitations:

- **Labor-Intensive**: Requires significant time and effort for monitoring and management.
- **Subjectivity**: Relies on visual observations and manual data entry, which can be inconsistent and prone to errors.

3. Modern Technologies for Livestock Management and Health Monitoring
IoT and Smart Sensors:
Definition:

- **IoT**: A network of interconnected devices that collect and exchange data. In livestock management, IoT devices include sensors that monitor various aspects of animal health and environment.

Key Components:

- **Wearable Sensors**: Devices worn by livestock to monitor health indicators such as temperature, heart rate, and activity levels.
- **Environmental Sensors**: Measure factors such as temperature, humidity, and ammonia levels in animal housing.

Applications:

- **Health Monitoring**: Continuous monitoring of vital signs and behavior to detect health issues early.
- **Environmental Management**: Ensures optimal living conditions by monitoring and controlling environmental factors.

Benefits:

- **Real-Time Data**: Provides immediate data on animal health and environmental conditions.
- **Early Detection**: Facilitates early detection of health issues and environmental problems.

Challenges:

- **Cost**: Initial setup and maintenance of IoT systems can be expensive.
- **Data Integration**: Requires integration of data from multiple sources for comprehensive analysis.

AI and Machine Learning:
Definition:

- **AI**: Artificial Intelligence involves simulating human intelligence processes by machines, including machine learning for pattern recognition and predictive analytics.

Key Components:

- **Predictive Models**: AI models analyze data to predict health issues, reproductive cycles, and productivity trends.
- **Behavior Analysis**: Machine learning algorithms analyze behavioral data to identify anomalies and potential health problems.

Applications:

- **Health Predictions**: Predicts potential health issues based on historical data and current observations.
- **Productivity Optimization**: Analyzes data to optimize feeding, breeding, and management practices.

Benefits:

- **Enhanced Accuracy**: Improves the accuracy of health predictions and management decisions.
- **Proactive Management**: Allows for proactive interventions based on predictive insights.

Challenges:

- **Data Quality**: Requires high-quality data for effective modeling and predictions.
- **Complexity**: Developing and implementing AI models can be complex and require specialized knowledge.

Data Analytics and Big Data:
Definition:

- **Data Analytics**: The process of examining large datasets to uncover patterns, trends, and insights. Big data involves managing and analyzing vast amounts of information.

Key Components:

- **Data Collection**: Gathering data from various sources, including sensors, records, and environmental observations.
- **Data Analysis**: Using statistical and machine learning techniques to analyze data and derive actionable insights.

Applications:

- **Health Monitoring**: Analyzes health data to identify trends and potential issues.
- **Management Decisions**: Supports decision-making by providing insights into livestock health, productivity, and welfare.

Benefits:

- **Comprehensive Insights**: Provides a holistic view of livestock health and management practices.
- **Informed Decisions**: Enhances decision-making with data-driven insights and recommendations.

Challenges:

- **Data Management**: Requires robust systems for managing and processing large datasets.
- **Expertise**: Analyzing big data requires specialized knowledge and skills.

Robotics and Automation:
Definition:

- **Robotics**: The use of automated machines and robots to perform tasks traditionally done by humans. In livestock management, robotics can assist with feeding, milking, and health monitoring.

Key Components:

- **Automated Feeders**: Robots that dispense feed based on pre-programmed schedules and animal needs.
- **Milking Robots**: Automated systems for milking dairy cattle, improving efficiency and consistency.

Applications:

- **Feeding**: Automates the feeding process, ensuring consistent and accurate feed distribution.
- **Health Monitoring**: Uses robotic systems to monitor animal health and perform routine checks.

Benefits:

- **Efficiency**: Increases efficiency and consistency in livestock management tasks.
- **Labor Savings**: Reduces the need for manual labor and frees up time for other activities.

Challenges:

- **Cost**: High initial investment and maintenance costs for robotic systems.
- **Integration**: Requires integration with existing management systems and practices.

Blockchain Technology:
Definition:

- **Blockchain**: A decentralized and secure digital ledger that records transactions across a distributed network.

Key Components:

- **Data Integrity**: Ensures the integrity and traceability of data related to livestock health and management.
- **Smart Contracts**: Automated contracts that execute transactions based on predefined conditions.

Applications:

- **Traceability**: Provides transparent and tamper-proof records of livestock health, breeding, and movement.
- **Data Security**: Protects sensitive health and management data from tampering and unauthorized access.

Benefits:

- **Transparency**: Enhances transparency and accountability in livestock management.
- **Data Security**: Provides secure and reliable data storage and sharing.

Challenges:

- **Complexity**: Implementing blockchain technology can be complex and require significant technical expertise.
- **Cost**: May involve high initial setup and integration costs.

Livestock management and health monitoring are crucial for ensuring the productivity and welfare of livestock. Modern technologies, including IoT, AI, data analytics, robotics, and blockchain, are revolutionizing these practices, providing more accurate, efficient, and proactive solutions. While these technologies offer significant benefits, such as enhanced accuracy, real-time data, and improved efficiency, they also present challenges related to cost, data management, and integration. Adopting these technologies can lead to more effective livestock management, better animal health, and increased productivity, contributing to the overall success and sustainability of livestock farming.

Pest and Weed Control

Effective pest and weed control is essential for maintaining crop health, maximizing yields, and ensuring sustainable agricultural practices. Advances in technology, including AI, IoT, and remote sensing, are transforming how pests and weeds are managed, offering innovative solutions for early detection, precise targeting, and efficient control.

1. Importance of Pest and Weed Control

Definitions:

- **Pest Control**: The management and elimination of organisms that harm crops, including insects, rodents, and other pests.
- **Weed Control**: The management of unwanted plants that compete with crops for resources such as nutrients, water, and sunlight.

Key Objectives:

- **Protect Crop Yield**: Prevent pests and weeds from reducing crop productivity and quality.
- **Minimize Crop Damage**: Reduce the physical damage caused by pests and competition from weeds.
- **Sustainable Practices**: Implement practices that minimize environmental impact and promote long-term agricultural health.

Benefits:

- **Increased Productivity**: Enhances crop yield and quality by controlling harmful organisms.

- **Reduced Losses**: Minimizes economic losses due to pest and weed damage.
- **Environmental Protection**: Promotes the use of sustainable methods to protect the environment.

2. Traditional Methods of Pest and Weed Control
Mechanical Control:

- **Manual Removal**: Hand weeding and physical removal of pests.
- **Traps and Barriers**: Using traps and physical barriers to control pest populations.

Chemical Control:

- **Pesticides**: Application of chemical substances to kill or repel pests.
- **Herbicides**: Chemicals used to control or eliminate weeds.

Biological Control:

- **Natural Predators**: Introducing or encouraging natural enemies of pests, such as ladybugs for aphid control.
- **Biopesticides**: Use of natural organisms or their products to control pests and diseases.

Limitations:

- **Labor-Intensive**: Mechanical and manual methods require significant labor and effort.
- **Environmental Impact**: Chemical control methods can lead to environmental pollution and resistance development.
- **Limited Scope**: Traditional methods may not be effective for all types of pests and weeds.

3. Modern Technologies for Pest and Weed Control
IoT and Smart Sensors:
Definition:

- **IoT**: A network of interconnected devices that collect and exchange data. In pest and weed control, IoT devices include sensors that monitor pest and weed activity.

Key Components:

- **Pest Sensors**: Devices that detect the presence of pests based on environmental conditions or physical traps.
- **Weed Sensors**: Sensors that identify and monitor weed growth in fields.

Applications:

- **Early Detection**: Identifies pest and weed issues early to enable timely intervention.
- **Real-Time Monitoring**: Provides continuous data on pest and weed activity for informed decision-making.

Benefits:

- **Timely Intervention**: Allows for early and targeted control measures.
- **Data-Driven Decisions**: Supports decisions based on real-time data and trends.

Challenges:

- **Cost**: Initial setup and maintenance of IoT systems can be expensive.
- **Data Integration**: Requires integration of data from multiple sensors for effective management.

AI and Machine Learning:
Definition:

- **AI**: Artificial Intelligence involves simulating human intelligence processes by machines, including machine learning for pattern recognition and predictive analytics.

Key Components:

- **Predictive Models**: AI models predict pest and weed outbreaks based on historical data and current conditions.
- **Image Recognition**: Machine learning algorithms analyze images to identify pests and weeds.

Applications:

- **Pest and Weed Identification**: Uses image recognition to accurately identify pests and weeds from photos or video feeds.
- **Predictive Analytics**: Forecasts pest and weed outbreaks based on environmental conditions and historical data.

Benefits:

- **Accuracy**: Enhances the precision of pest and weed identification and management.
- **Proactive Management**: Enables proactive measures based on predictive insights.

Challenges:

- **Data Quality**: Requires high-quality data for effective modeling and predictions.
- **Complexity**: Developing and implementing AI models can be complex and require specialized knowledge.

Remote Sensing and Satellite Imagery:
Definition:

- **Remote Sensing**: The use of satellite or aerial imagery to collect data about crops and fields from a distance.

Key Components:

- **Satellite Imagery**: Provides large-scale observations of crop conditions, pest infestations, and weed growth.
- **Drones**: Offer high-resolution, localized imagery for detailed analysis.

Applications:

- **Pest and Weed Mapping**: Identifies and maps pest and weed infestations over large areas.
- **Monitoring**: Tracks changes in pest and weed populations over time.

Benefits:

- **Broad Coverage**: Offers extensive data across large areas, improving management efforts.
- **Real-Time Data**: Provides up-to-date information on pest and weed conditions.

Challenges:

- **Cost**: High-resolution imagery and remote sensing equipment can be expensive.
- **Data Processing**: Requires specialized software and expertise to analyze and interpret data.

Robotics and Automation:
Definition:

- **Robotics**: The use of automated machines and robots to perform tasks traditionally done by humans. In pest and weed control, robotics can assist with targeted applications of control measures.

Key Components:

- **Automated Sprayers**: Robots that apply pesticides or herbicides precisely where needed.
- **Weeding Robots**: Automated systems that remove weeds without harming crops.

Applications:

- **Precision Application**: Targets specific areas for pesticide or herbicide application, reducing waste and environmental impact.

- **Efficient Weeding**: Automates the process of weed removal, improving efficiency and consistency.

Benefits:

- **Efficiency**: Increases efficiency and reduces labor in pest and weed control tasks.
- **Precision**: Minimizes the use of chemicals and improves targeting.

Challenges:

- **Cost**: High initial investment and maintenance costs for robotic systems.
- **Integration**: Requires integration with existing management practices and systems.

Data Analytics and Big Data:
Definition:

- **Data Analytics**: The process of examining large datasets to uncover patterns, trends, and insights. Big data involves managing and analyzing vast amounts of information.

Key Components:

- **Data Collection**: Gathering data from various sources, including sensors, satellite imagery, and historical records.
- **Data Analysis**: Using statistical and machine learning techniques to analyze data and derive actionable insights.

Applications:

- **Pest and Weed Management**: Analyzes data to identify patterns and trends in pest and weed populations.
- **Decision Support**: Provides insights for effective pest and weed control strategies.

Benefits:

- **Comprehensive Insights**: Offers a holistic view of pest and weed dynamics.
- **Informed Decisions**: Enhances decision-making with data-driven insights and recommendations.

Challenges:

- **Data Management**: Requires robust systems for managing and processing large datasets.
- **Expertise**: Analyzing big data requires specialized knowledge and skills.

Pest and weed control is a critical aspect of agricultural management, impacting crop health, productivity, and sustainability. Modern technologies, including IoT, AI, remote sensing, robotics, and data analytics, are revolutionizing how pests and weeds are managed. These technologies offer significant benefits such as enhanced accuracy, real-time monitoring, and efficient control measures. However, they also present challenges related to cost, data management, and integration. Adopting these technologies can lead to more effective and sustainable pest and weed control practices, ultimately improving crop yields and reducing environmental impact.

Market Price Forecasting and Decision Support Systems

Market price forecasting and decision support systems are crucial for optimizing agricultural production, enhancing profitability, and making informed decisions in the agricultural sector. These systems leverage technology to predict market trends, assist in decision-making, and improve overall efficiency in agriculture.

1. Importance of Market Price Forecasting
Definition:

- **Market Price Forecasting**: The process of predicting future prices of agricultural products based on various factors, including historical data, market trends, and economic indicators.

Key Objectives:

- **Optimize Sales**: Enable farmers and stakeholders to plan and time their sales for maximum profitability.

- **Risk Management**: Help manage price volatility and financial risk associated with market fluctuations.
- **Strategic Planning**: Assist in making strategic decisions related to production, marketing, and investments.

Benefits:

- **Improved Profitability**: Helps farmers and businesses maximize returns by timing sales according to market conditions.
- **Informed Decisions**: Provides insights for better decision-making regarding production levels, storage, and marketing strategies.
- **Reduced Risk**: Mitigates the impact of market volatility on income and financial stability.

2. Traditional Methods of Price Forecasting
Historical Analysis:

- **Trend Analysis**: Examines historical price data to identify patterns and trends.
- **Seasonal Analysis**: Considers seasonal variations in prices based on historical data.

Market Surveys:

- **Market Intelligence**: Collects data from market reports, auctions, and trade publications.
- **Expert Opinions**: Relies on insights and predictions from market analysts and industry experts.

Limitations:

- **Lagging Indicators**: Historical data may not accurately reflect current market conditions or future trends.
- **Limited Scope**: Traditional methods may not account for all factors affecting market prices, such as global events or technological changes.

3. Modern Technologies for Market Price Forecasting
Machine Learning and AI:

Definition:

- **Machine Learning**: A subset of AI that involves training algorithms to recognize patterns and make predictions based on data. In market price forecasting, machine learning models analyze historical and real-time data to predict future prices.

Key Components:

- **Predictive Models**: Algorithms that analyze historical data, market trends, and other factors to forecast future prices.
- **Sentiment Analysis**: Uses natural language processing to gauge market sentiment from news articles, social media, and reports.

Applications:

- **Price Prediction**: Provides forecasts of future prices based on historical data and real-time inputs.
- **Trend Analysis**: Identifies emerging trends and patterns in market data.

Benefits:

- **Accuracy**: Enhances the accuracy of price predictions through sophisticated algorithms.
- **Adaptability**: Adjusts predictions based on real-time data and changing conditions.

Challenges:

- **Data Quality**: Requires high-quality data for effective modeling and predictions.
- **Complexity**: Developing and implementing machine learning models can be complex and require specialized expertise.

Big Data Analytics:
Definition:

- **Big Data Analytics**: The process of analyzing large and complex datasets to uncover patterns, trends, and insights. In market price forecasting, big data analytics involves processing vast amounts of data from various sources.

Key Components:

- **Data Integration**: Combining data from multiple sources, including historical prices, weather patterns, and economic indicators.
- **Advanced Analytics**: Employs statistical and machine learning techniques to analyze data and generate forecasts.

Applications:

- **Market Analysis**: Provides comprehensive insights into market trends and price dynamics.
- **Forecasting**: Enhances the accuracy of price forecasts through analysis of large datasets.

Benefits:

- **Comprehensive Insights**: Offers a detailed view of market trends and factors affecting prices.
- **Informed Decisions**: Supports better decision-making with data-driven insights.

Challenges:

- **Data Management**: Requires robust systems for managing and processing large volumes of data.
- **Expertise**: Analyzing big data requires specialized knowledge and skills.

Decision Support Systems (DSS):
Definition:

- **Decision Support Systems**: Computer-based systems that assist in decision-making by providing relevant data, models, and analytical tools.

Key Components:

- **Data Management**: Stores and manages data related to market prices, production, and economic indicators.
- **Analytical Tools**: Provides tools for analyzing data, generating forecasts, and evaluating different scenarios.

Applications:

- **Scenario Analysis**: Allows users to explore different scenarios and their potential impact on prices and profitability.
- **Strategic Planning**: Supports decision-making related to production, marketing, and investment strategies.

Benefits:

- **Enhanced Decision-Making**: Provides valuable insights and tools for making informed decisions.
- **Scenario Evaluation**: Helps evaluate the potential impact of different strategies and scenarios.

Challenges:

- **Integration**: Requires integration with existing systems and data sources.
- **User Training**: Users need to be trained to effectively use DSS tools and interpret results.

IoT and Real-Time Data:
Definition:

- **IoT**: A network of interconnected devices that collect and exchange data. In market price forecasting, IoT devices can provide real-time data on various factors affecting prices.

Key Components:

- **Sensors**: Devices that collect data on weather, soil conditions, and crop status.
- **Data Streams**: Real-time data streams from markets, sensors, and other sources.

Applications:

- **Real-Time Monitoring**: Provides up-to-date information on factors affecting market prices.
- **Dynamic Forecasting**: Adjusts forecasts based on real-time data and changing conditions.

Benefits:

- **Timely Insights**: Offers immediate data for more accurate and timely forecasts.
- **Dynamic Adjustments**: Allows for adjustments to forecasts based on real-time information.

Challenges:

- **Data Integration**: Requires integration of real-time data with forecasting models.
- **Data Management**: Managing and processing real-time data can be challenging.

Market price forecasting and decision support systems play a vital role in optimizing agricultural production and profitability. Modern technologies, including machine learning, big data analytics, decision support systems, and IoT, offer advanced solutions for predicting market trends, analyzing data, and making informed decisions. While these technologies provide significant benefits such as improved accuracy, real-time insights, and enhanced decision-making, they also present challenges related to data quality, complexity, and integration. Adopting these technologies can lead to more effective and efficient market price forecasting, ultimately supporting better agricultural practices and improved financial outcomes.

CHAPTER V

Case Studies of AI Implementation in India

Success Stories of AI in Crop Management

AI has revolutionized crop management by providing innovative solutions for optimizing various aspects of agriculture, from planting and cultivation to harvesting and post-harvest processing. Here are some notable success stories where AI has made a significant impact on crop management:

1. IBM's Watson Decision Platform for Agriculture

Overview: IBM's Watson Decision Platform for Agriculture integrates AI, IoT, and blockchain to provide comprehensive solutions for crop management. This platform leverages data from various sources, including weather forecasts, soil conditions, and satellite imagery, to offer actionable insights for farmers.

Key Features:

- **Predictive Analytics**: Uses machine learning algorithms to forecast weather patterns, disease outbreaks, and pest invasions.
- **Decision Support**: Provides recommendations on irrigation, fertilization, and pest control based on real-time data.
- **Data Integration**: Combines data from sensors, drones, and satellites to offer a holistic view of crop health and management.

Success Story: A pilot project in India utilized IBM's Watson to improve wheat yields. By analyzing weather data and soil conditions, the system recommended optimal planting times and irrigation schedules. Farmers who implemented these recommendations saw a significant increase in yield and a reduction in water usage.

2. The Climate Corporation's Climate FieldView

Overview: The Climate Corporation's Climate FieldView is a digital agriculture platform that uses AI to provide insights into crop health and performance. The platform offers tools for monitoring field conditions, predicting yields, and optimizing input usage.

Key Features:

- **Field Monitoring**: Utilizes satellite imagery and sensor data to track crop health and growth.
- **Yield Prediction**: AI models predict crop yields based on historical data and current conditions.
- **Input Optimization**: Recommends the optimal amount of fertilizers, pesticides, and water for each field.

Success Story: In the United States, Climate FieldView was used by a large-scale corn producer to optimize fertilizer application. By analyzing soil data and weather forecasts, the platform suggested precise fertilizer rates, leading to a 10% increase in corn yield and a reduction in fertilizer costs.

3. John Deere's See & Spray Technology

Overview: John Deere's See & Spray technology uses computer vision and AI to identify and target weeds in real-time. The system is integrated into John Deere's sprayers and enables precise application of herbicides.

Key Features:

- **Weed Detection**: AI algorithms analyze camera images to distinguish between crops and weeds.
- **Targeted Application**: Herbicides are applied only to the weeds, reducing chemical usage and minimizing damage to crops.
- **Real-Time Processing**: The system processes images and makes decisions in real-time as the sprayer moves through the field.

Success Story: A cotton farmer in Texas implemented See & Spray technology to manage weed populations. The AI system significantly reduced herbicide use, leading to cost savings and less environmental impact. The farmer also reported improved cotton yields due to reduced competition from weeds.

4. Taranis' Aerial Crop Monitoring

Overview: Taranis uses AI-powered aerial imagery to monitor crop health and detect issues such as pests, diseases, and nutrient deficiencies. The platform combines high-resolution drone imagery with AI analysis to provide detailed insights.

Key Features:

- **Aerial Imagery**: Captures high-resolution images of crops using drones.

- **AI Analysis**: AI algorithms analyze the images to detect signs of stress, disease, or pest infestations.
- **Actionable Insights**: Provides recommendations for targeted interventions based on analysis.

Success Story: In Brazil, Taranis was used by a soybean producer to monitor fields for early signs of pests and diseases. The AI system identified problems that were not visible to the naked eye, allowing for early intervention. The result was a significant reduction in crop losses and an improvement in overall yield.

5. CropX's Soil Sensor Technology

Overview: CropX offers AI-powered soil sensor technology that provides real-time data on soil moisture, temperature, and nutrient levels. The system uses AI to analyze the data and offer recommendations for irrigation and fertilization.

Key Features:

- **Soil Sensors**: Monitors soil conditions in real-time using wireless sensors.
- **AI Analysis**: Processes sensor data to determine optimal irrigation and fertilization strategies.
- **Automated Recommendations**: Provides actionable insights for improving soil health and crop performance.

Success Story: A vineyard in California adopted CropX's soil sensor technology to manage irrigation more efficiently. The AI system recommended precise irrigation schedules based on soil moisture levels and weather forecasts. The vineyard experienced a 20% reduction in water usage and improved grape quality.

AI is transforming crop management by offering innovative solutions for monitoring, optimizing, and enhancing agricultural practices. Success stories from IBM, Climate Corporation, John Deere, Taranis, and CropX demonstrate the significant benefits of AI, including increased yields, reduced costs, and improved sustainability. These technologies not only enhance productivity but also contribute to more efficient and environmentally friendly farming practices. As AI continues to evolve, its role in crop management is likely to expand, offering even greater opportunities for innovation and improvement in agriculture.

AI in Dairy Farming: Innovations and Impact

Artificial Intelligence (AI) has introduced transformative changes in dairy farming, enhancing productivity, animal health, and operational efficiency. By leveraging advanced technologies, dairy farms can optimize various aspects of milk production, from herd management to milk quality monitoring. Here's an overview of key innovations and their impact on dairy farming:

1. Automated Milking Systems

Overview: Automated milking systems (AMS), also known as robotic milking systems, use AI to manage the milking process. These systems include robots that perform milking tasks with minimal human intervention.

Key Features:

- **Robotic Milkers**: Machines equipped with AI-powered sensors and robotics that identify and attach to the cow's udder.
- **Data Analysis**: Monitors milk production, udder health, and cow behavior in real-time.
- **Automatic Cleaning**: Ensures hygiene through automated cleaning and sanitizing of equipment.

Impact:

- **Increased Efficiency**: Reduces labor costs and increases milking efficiency by allowing cows to be milked multiple times a day based on their needs.
- **Enhanced Milk Quality**: Provides consistent milking conditions, leading to higher milk quality and reduced risk of contamination.
- **Improved Animal Welfare**: Minimizes stress on cows by allowing them to be milked at their own convenience.

2. AI-Driven Herd Management

Overview: AI-powered herd management systems analyze data related to cow health, behavior, and productivity. These systems use sensors and machine learning algorithms to provide actionable insights.

Key Features:

- **Health Monitoring**: AI systems track vital signs, activity levels, and behavioral patterns to detect health issues early.
- **Behavioral Analysis**: Monitors social interactions and feeding patterns to identify issues such as lameness or estrus.
- **Productivity Tracking**: Analyzes milk yield and quality data to optimize feeding and breeding practices.

Impact:

- **Early Disease Detection**: Enables early diagnosis of health issues, reducing the need for costly treatments and minimizing herd losses.
- **Optimized Feeding**: Tailors feeding programs based on individual cow needs, improving milk production and reducing waste.
- **Efficient Breeding**: Uses data to make informed breeding decisions, leading to better herd genetics and increased productivity.

3. AI in Milk Quality Testing

Overview: AI technologies are used to test and monitor milk quality. These systems analyze various parameters such as fat content, protein levels, and somatic cell counts to ensure high-quality milk.

Key Features:

- **Automated Testing**: AI-powered devices conduct continuous and automated milk quality testing.
- **Real-Time Data**: Provides immediate feedback on milk quality parameters.
- **Predictive Analytics**: Uses historical data to predict potential quality issues and recommend adjustments.

Impact:

- **Consistent Quality**: Ensures milk meets quality standards, reducing the risk of spoilage and contamination.
- **Regulatory Compliance**: Helps dairy farms comply with food safety regulations by providing accurate quality metrics.
- **Consumer Confidence**: Enhances consumer trust by ensuring high-quality and safe milk products.

4. Precision Feeding

Overview: Precision feeding uses AI to optimize the nutrition of dairy cattle. By analyzing individual cow data, these systems provide tailored feeding solutions to improve milk production and herd health.

Key Features:

- **Nutrient Analysis**: AI analyzes feed composition and cow nutritional needs.
- **Customized Rations**: Provides recommendations for customized feed rations based on individual cow requirements.
- **Feed Efficiency**: Monitors feed intake and utilization to optimize feeding strategies.

Impact:

- **Enhanced Productivity**: Improves milk yield and quality by providing the right nutrients at the right time.
- **Reduced Costs**: Minimizes feed waste and lowers feed costs through precise rationing.
- **Improved Health**: Supports better overall health and performance of the herd by ensuring balanced nutrition.

5. AI-Enhanced Breeding Programs

Overview: AI-driven breeding programs use genetic data and predictive analytics to improve herd genetics and productivity. These systems assist in selecting the best breeding candidates based on desired traits.

Key Features:

- **Genetic Analysis**: AI analyzes genetic information to identify desirable traits and genetic markers.
- **Predictive Modeling**: Uses models to predict the outcomes of breeding decisions.
- **Data Integration**: Integrates data from various sources, including performance records and genomic information.

Impact:

- **Improved Genetics**: Enhances herd genetics by selecting superior breeding candidates, leading to better milk production and disease resistance.
- **Increased Efficiency**: Reduces the time and resources needed for breeding programs by providing data-driven insights.
- **Long-Term Benefits**: Contributes to sustainable and profitable dairy farming by improving herd quality over time.

6. AI-Powered Environmental Monitoring

Overview: AI systems are used to monitor and manage the environmental conditions of dairy farms. These systems track factors such as temperature, humidity, and air quality to ensure optimal conditions for cattle.

Key Features:

- **Environmental Sensors**: Monitors conditions such as temperature, humidity, and air quality.
- **AI Analysis**: Analyzes environmental data to provide recommendations for adjustments.
- **Automated Controls**: Adjusts environmental conditions based on real-time data.

Impact:

- **Enhanced Comfort**: Ensures optimal environmental conditions, improving animal comfort and reducing stress.
- **Energy Efficiency**: Optimizes the use of heating, cooling, and ventilation systems, reducing energy costs.
- **Health Benefits**: Reduces the risk of heat stress and respiratory issues in cattle.

AI innovations in dairy farming have led to significant improvements in productivity, animal health, and operational efficiency. Automated milking systems, AI-driven herd management, milk quality testing, precision feeding, enhanced breeding programs, and environmental monitoring are just a few examples of how AI is transforming the industry. These technologies not only enhance the efficiency and sustainability of dairy farming but also contribute to better animal welfare and improved milk quality. As AI continues to advance, its role in dairy farming is expected to expand, offering even greater opportunities for innovation and improvement.

AI-Powered Solutions for Smallholder Farmers

Smallholder farmers face unique challenges, including limited resources, access to technology, and knowledge. AI-powered solutions can provide significant benefits by improving productivity, efficiency, and decision-making in a way that is accessible and practical for smallholder farms. Here are some notable AI-powered solutions tailored for smallholder farmers:

1. AI-Driven Crop Recommendations

Overview: AI systems analyze local soil, climate, and crop data to provide personalized crop recommendations for smallholder farmers. These recommendations help farmers choose the most suitable crops for their specific conditions.

Key Features:

- **Data Analysis**: Uses AI to analyze soil health, climate patterns, and historical crop performance.
- **Personalized Recommendations**: Provides tailored crop suggestions based on the farmer's location and resources.
- **Adaptive Models**: Continuously updates recommendations based on new data and changing conditions.

Impact:

- **Increased Yield**: Helps farmers select crops that are well-suited to their environment, leading to better yields.
- **Resource Optimization**: Reduces the risk of crop failure and optimizes the use of inputs such as water and fertilizers.
- **Risk Reduction**: Minimizes the risks associated with crop selection and helps farmers make informed decisions.

2. AI-Powered Pest and Disease Detection

Overview: AI technologies use image recognition and machine learning to identify pests and diseases in crops. Farmers can use these tools to detect problems early and take timely action.

Key Features:

- **Image Recognition**: Analyzes photos of crops to identify signs of pests or diseases.
- **Real-Time Alerts**: Provides instant notifications when potential issues are detected.
- **Treatment Recommendations**: Suggests appropriate treatments or interventions based on the identified problems.

Impact:

- **Early Detection**: Enables early identification of pests and diseases, reducing the impact on crops.
- **Cost Savings**: Helps farmers avoid expensive treatments and minimize crop losses.
- **Improved Management**: Supports better pest and disease management through accurate and timely information.

3. AI-Enhanced Precision Agriculture

Overview: Precision agriculture technologies use AI to optimize the application of inputs such as water, fertilizers, and pesticides. These solutions help smallholder farmers manage their resources more efficiently.

Key Features:

- **Soil and Crop Sensors**: Monitors soil moisture, nutrient levels, and crop health.
- **AI Analysis**: Processes sensor data to provide recommendations for optimal input application.
- **Automated Controls**: Adjusts irrigation and fertilization based on real-time data.

Impact:

- **Increased Efficiency**: Reduces waste of resources and improves the effectiveness of inputs.
- **Higher Yields**: Enhances crop productivity by ensuring optimal growing conditions.
- **Environmental Benefits**: Minimizes the environmental impact of farming practices by reducing overuse of inputs.

4. Mobile-Based AI Apps

Overview: Mobile applications powered by AI offer smallholder farmers access to a range of tools and information. These apps provide valuable resources, such as weather forecasts, market prices, and farming advice.

Key Features:

- **Weather Forecasts**: Provides accurate weather predictions to help with planning and decision-making.
- **Market Prices**: Offers information on current market prices to assist with selling decisions.
- **Agricultural Advice**: Delivers tips and recommendations for crop management, pest control, and other farming practices.

Impact:

- **Improved Access**: Provides valuable information and tools directly to farmers' smartphones.
- **Enhanced Decision-Making**: Supports better decision-making with timely and relevant information.
- **Market Integration**: Helps farmers make informed decisions about when and where to sell their products.

5. AI for Financial and Risk Management

Overview: AI solutions assist smallholder farmers with financial planning and risk management. These tools help farmers manage their finances, access credit, and mitigate risks.

Key Features:

- **Financial Forecasting**: Uses AI to predict income and expenses based on farm data and market conditions.
- **Credit Scoring**: Assists with assessing creditworthiness and accessing loans or financial services.
- **Risk Assessment**: Evaluates risks such as weather events, crop failures, and market fluctuations.

Impact:

- **Financial Stability**: Helps farmers manage their finances more effectively and plan for future expenses.
- **Access to Credit**: Facilitates access to credit and financial services, supporting farm growth and development.
- **Risk Mitigation**: Reduces financial risks by providing insights and strategies for managing uncertainties.

6. AI-Driven Farm Management Platforms

Overview: Farm management platforms use AI to integrate various aspects of farm operations, providing a comprehensive solution for managing crops, livestock, and resources.

Key Features:

- **Integrated Management**: Combines data on crop production, livestock, and resource use into a single platform.
- **Decision Support**: Offers tools for planning, monitoring, and optimizing farm operations.
- **Data Analytics**: Provides insights and recommendations based on data collected from various sources.

Impact:

- **Streamlined Operations**: Simplifies farm management by integrating multiple aspects of farming into one platform.
- **Enhanced Efficiency**: Improves operational efficiency through data-driven insights and recommendations.
- **Better Planning**: Supports strategic planning and decision-making with comprehensive data analysis.

AI-powered solutions are transforming smallholder farming by providing tools and technologies that address specific challenges faced by these farmers. From crop recommendations and pest detection to precision agriculture and financial management, AI offers practical and impactful solutions that enhance productivity, efficiency, and decision-making. By making advanced technologies accessible and relevant to smallholder farmers, AI is helping to drive agricultural growth and sustainability in diverse farming environments.

Role of Startups in AI-Based Agricultural Solutions

Startups play a crucial role in advancing AI-based agricultural solutions by driving innovation, offering specialized technologies, and addressing specific needs within the agricultural sector. Their contributions can significantly enhance productivity, efficiency, and sustainability in farming practices. Here's an overview of how startups are influencing AI in agriculture:

1. Innovation and Technology Development

Overview: Startups are often at the forefront of technological innovation, developing cutting-edge AI solutions tailored to agriculture. They explore new technologies, create novel applications, and push the boundaries of what is possible in farming.

Key Contributions:

- **Novel Algorithms**: Develop new machine learning algorithms for better crop prediction, pest detection, and resource management.
- **Advanced Sensors**: Innovate in sensor technologies for real-time monitoring of soil health, weather conditions, and crop growth.
- **AI Platforms**: Create platforms that integrate various AI tools and technologies for comprehensive farm management.

Impact:

- **Technological Advancement**: Accelerates the development and adoption of advanced AI technologies in agriculture.
- **Competitive Edge**: Provides farmers with access to state-of-the-art tools and solutions that enhance their productivity and efficiency.

2. Addressing Specific Agricultural Challenges

Overview: Startups often focus on niche areas within agriculture, offering specialized solutions to address specific challenges faced by farmers. Their targeted approaches help solve particular problems effectively.

Key Contributions:

- **Pest and Disease Management**: Develop AI tools for early detection and management of pests and diseases tailored to regional crops and conditions.

- **Precision Agriculture**: Offer precision farming solutions that optimize input use and improve crop yield based on local data.
- **Supply Chain Optimization**: Create solutions that enhance the efficiency of agricultural supply chains, from production to market.

Impact:

- **Targeted Solutions**: Provides farmers with tools that address specific issues, improving overall farm management.
- **Efficiency Gains**: Enhances efficiency in areas such as pest control, irrigation, and logistics through specialized technologies.

3. Making AI Accessible to Smallholder Farmers

Overview: Startups are working to make AI technologies more accessible and affordable for smallholder farmers, who may have limited resources and access to advanced tools.

Key Contributions:

- **Affordable Solutions**: Develop cost-effective AI tools and platforms that are within the budget of smallholder farmers.
- **Mobile Applications**: Create user-friendly mobile apps that provide AI-powered insights and recommendations directly to farmers' smartphones.
- **Training and Support**: Offer training and support to help farmers understand and effectively use AI technologies.

Impact:

- **Increased Accessibility**: Expands the reach of AI technologies to smallholder farmers, improving their productivity and sustainability.
- **Empowerment**: Empowers farmers with tools and knowledge to make informed decisions and manage their farms more effectively.

4. Collaboration with Research and Development Institutions

Overview: Many startups collaborate with research institutions, universities, and agricultural organizations to develop and validate their AI solutions. These partnerships help integrate cutting-edge research with practical applications.

Key Contributions:

- **Joint Research Projects**: Engage in collaborative research to develop new AI applications and technologies for agriculture.
- **Field Trials**: Conduct field trials in partnership with research institutions to test and refine AI solutions.
- **Knowledge Sharing**: Benefit from academic expertise and research findings to enhance the effectiveness of their technologies.

Impact:

- **Enhanced Credibility**: Leverages academic research to validate and improve AI solutions, increasing their credibility and effectiveness.
- **Accelerated Development**: Speeds up the development and adoption of new technologies through collaborative efforts.

5. Driving Sustainable Agricultural Practices

Overview: Startups are increasingly focusing on sustainability, developing AI solutions that promote environmentally friendly and sustainable farming practices.

Key Contributions:

- **Resource Management**: Create AI tools that optimize the use of water, fertilizers, and pesticides, reducing waste and environmental impact.
- **Climate Adaptation**: Develop solutions that help farmers adapt to climate change by providing insights into weather patterns and crop resilience.
- **Sustainable Practices**: Promote sustainable farming practices through AI-driven recommendations and monitoring.

Impact:

- **Environmental Benefits**: Supports sustainable agriculture by reducing the environmental footprint of farming practices.
- **Long-Term Viability**: Contributes to the long-term viability of farming by promoting practices that are environmentally friendly and resource-efficient.

6. Facilitating Market Access and Financial Services

Overview: Startups are creating AI solutions that help farmers access markets and financial services, improving their economic stability and market competitiveness.

Key Contributions:

- **Market Intelligence**: Provide AI-powered insights into market prices, demand trends, and buyer preferences.
- **Financial Inclusion**: Develop platforms that facilitate access to credit, insurance, and financial services tailored to farmers' needs.
- **E-Commerce Platforms**: Create digital marketplaces that connect farmers directly with buyers, reducing intermediaries and improving profitability.

Impact:

- **Market Access**: Enhances farmers' ability to access and compete in markets, improving their income and economic stability.
- **Financial Empowerment**: Provides farmers with financial tools and services that support their growth and development.

Startups are playing a vital role in advancing AI-based agricultural solutions by driving innovation, addressing specific challenges, and making technology accessible to diverse farming communities. Their contributions span from developing novel technologies to enhancing sustainability and financial access, providing valuable tools and resources that help farmers improve productivity, efficiency, and overall farm management. As the agricultural sector continues to evolve, startups will remain a key driver of progress, shaping the future of AI in agriculture.

Government Initiatives and Public-Private Partnerships in AI-Based Agricultural Solutions

Government initiatives and public-private partnerships play a crucial role in the advancement and deployment of AI-based solutions in agriculture. These collaborations help facilitate the development, adoption, and scaling of innovative technologies that address agricultural challenges and enhance productivity. Here's an overview of key government initiatives and public-private partnerships that support AI in agriculture:

1. Government Initiatives

Overview: Governments around the world are recognizing the potential of AI to transform agriculture and are implementing various initiatives to promote its development and application. These initiatives often include funding, policy support, and infrastructure development.

Key Initiatives:

- **Digital India Program**:

  - **Overview**: Launched by the Government of India to enhance digital infrastructure and promote digital literacy across various sectors, including agriculture.
  - **AI Focus**: Supports the development and deployment of digital tools and AI technologies for farmers, including e-agriculture platforms and data-driven solutions.
  - **Impact**: Improves access to digital services and information for farmers, facilitating the adoption of AI technologies.

- **Pradhan Mantri Krishi Sinchai Yojana (PMKSY)**:

  - **Overview**: Aims to enhance irrigation infrastructure and promote water use efficiency in agriculture.
  - **AI Focus**: Integrates AI technologies for efficient water management and precision irrigation.
  - **Impact**: Enhances water resource management and improves crop yields through AI-driven irrigation solutions.

- **National Agriculture Market (eNAM)**:

  - **Overview**: A pan-India electronic trading platform for agricultural commodities.
  - **AI Focus**: Uses AI to analyze market trends, price fluctuations, and demand patterns.
  - **Impact**: Facilitates better market access and price discovery for farmers through data-driven insights.

- **Kisan Samadhan Portal**:

- Overview: A platform for addressing farmers' grievances and providing solutions.
- AI Focus: Incorporates AI tools for analyzing feedback and improving response mechanisms.
- Impact: Enhances government responsiveness and support for farmers through AI-driven analysis.

- **Atal Innovation Mission (AIM):**

  - Overview: Supports innovation and entrepreneurship across various sectors, including agriculture.
  - AI Focus: Provides funding and support for startups developing AI-based agricultural solutions.
  - Impact: Encourages innovation and accelerates the development of AI technologies for agriculture.

2. Public-Private Partnerships (PPP)

Overview: Public-private partnerships (PPPs) leverage the strengths of both government and private sector organizations to advance AI in agriculture. These collaborations often focus on research, technology development, and implementation.

Key Partnerships:

- **Agricultural Technology Development Centers:**

  - Overview: Collaborative centers involving government agencies, private companies, and research institutions.
  - AI Focus: Develop and test AI technologies for various agricultural applications, including precision farming and crop management.
  - Impact: Accelerates the development and adoption of innovative AI solutions through collaborative efforts.

- **AgriTech Startups Incubators:**

  - Overview: Incubators supported by both public and private sectors to nurture AgriTech startups.
  - AI Focus: Provide resources, mentorship, and funding for startups developing AI-based agricultural technologies.

- ○ **Impact**: Supports the growth of innovative startups and accelerates the commercialization of AI solutions in agriculture.

- **Research and Development (R&D) Collaborations**:

  - ○ **Overview**: Partnerships between government research institutions and private companies.
  - ○ **AI Focus**: Conduct joint research on AI applications in agriculture, including crop monitoring, soil management, and pest control.
  - ○ **Impact**: Combines expertise and resources to advance AI research and develop practical solutions for farmers.

- **Smart Agriculture Projects**:

  - ○ **Overview**: Government-backed projects that partner with technology companies to implement smart agriculture solutions.
  - ○ **AI Focus**: Deploy AI-powered systems for precision farming, irrigation management, and yield forecasting.
  - ○ **Impact**: Demonstrates the effectiveness of AI technologies and provides scalable solutions for farmers.

- **AI-Driven Agricultural Platforms**:

  - ○ **Overview**: Collaborations between government agencies and tech companies to create comprehensive agricultural platforms.
  - ○ **AI Focus**: Integrate AI tools for data analytics, market access, and farm management.
  - ○ **Impact**: Provides farmers with a one-stop solution for accessing various AI-powered agricultural services.

3. Funding and Support Programs

Overview: Government and private entities provide funding and support programs to encourage the development and deployment of AI technologies in agriculture.

Key Programs:

- **Agricultural Innovation Grants**:

- ◦ **Overview**: Grants provided by government agencies and private foundations to support AI research and development in agriculture.
- ◦ **AI Focus**: Fund projects that develop and test new AI technologies for agricultural applications.
- ◦ **Impact**: Provides financial support to researchers and innovators working on AI solutions.

- **Technology Transfer Programs**:

  - ◦ **Overview**: Programs that facilitate the transfer of technology from research institutions to the market.
  - ◦ **AI Focus**: Support the commercialization of AI technologies developed through public-private partnerships.
  - ◦ **Impact**: Bridges the gap between research and practical application, accelerating the deployment of AI solutions.

- **Agri-Tech Investment Funds**:

  - ◦ **Overview**: Investment funds focused on supporting AgriTech startups and innovations.
  - ◦ **AI Focus**: Invest in startups developing AI-based solutions for agriculture.
  - ◦ **Impact**: Provides capital for startups to scale their technologies and reach broader markets.

Government initiatives and public-private partnerships are essential for advancing AI-based agricultural solutions. By providing funding, policy support, and collaborative opportunities, these efforts help drive innovation, improve technology adoption, and address critical challenges in agriculture. Through these collaborations, AI technologies can be effectively developed and implemented, enhancing productivity, efficiency, and sustainability in the agricultural sector.

CHAPTER VI

Challenges in Adopting AI in Indian Agriculture

Technological Barriers in AI-Based Agricultural Solutions

Despite the potential of AI to revolutionize agriculture, several technological barriers impede its widespread adoption and effectiveness. These barriers can limit the development, deployment, and utilization of AI technologies in farming. Here's an overview of the key technological barriers:

1. Data Quality and Availability

Overview: AI systems rely heavily on data to make accurate predictions and decisions. In agriculture, the quality and availability of data can be inconsistent, affecting the performance of AI solutions.

Challenges:

- **Incomplete Data**: Often, data collected from farms are incomplete or lack the granularity needed for effective AI models.
- **Data Integration**: Difficulty in integrating data from various sources (e.g., sensors, satellite imagery) into a cohesive format for AI analysis.
- **Data Privacy**: Concerns about sharing and accessing sensitive data, especially in regions with stringent data protection regulations.

Impact:

- **Inaccurate Models**: Poor quality or insufficient data can lead to inaccurate predictions and unreliable AI systems.
- **Limited Insights**: Incomplete data limits the ability to derive comprehensive insights and actionable recommendations.

2. Infrastructure and Connectivity Issues

Overview: The effective implementation of AI solutions in agriculture requires robust infrastructure and connectivity, which can be lacking in rural and remote areas.

Challenges:

- **Internet Connectivity**: Limited or unreliable internet access in rural areas hinders the use of cloud-based AI services and real-time data processing.
- **Power Supply**: Inconsistent power supply can affect the operation of AI-powered devices and sensors.
- **Technological Infrastructure**: Insufficient technological infrastructure, such as advanced computing resources, can limit the deployment of AI solutions.

Impact:

- **Operational Disruptions**: Connectivity and infrastructure issues can disrupt the functioning of AI systems and limit their effectiveness.
- **Increased Costs**: Poor infrastructure can increase the costs associated with implementing and maintaining AI technologies.

3. High Cost of Technology

Overview: The cost of developing, implementing, and maintaining AI technologies can be prohibitively high, especially for smallholder farmers and developing regions.

Challenges:

- **Development Costs**: High costs associated with the development of AI algorithms, software, and hardware.
- **Implementation Costs**: Expenses related to installing and integrating AI systems on farms.
- **Maintenance Costs**: Ongoing costs for maintaining and updating AI technologies and supporting infrastructure.

Impact:

- **Limited Adoption**: High costs can deter farmers from adopting AI technologies, especially in low-income regions.
- **Economic Disparities**: Increases the gap between large-scale and small-scale farmers in accessing advanced technologies.

4. Technical Expertise and Training

Overview: The effective use of AI technologies requires a certain level of technical expertise, which can be a barrier in regions where such expertise is scarce.

Challenges:

- **Skill Gaps**: Lack of trained personnel who can develop, implement, and manage AI systems.
- **Training Programs**: Limited availability of training programs to educate farmers and agricultural professionals about AI technologies.
- **Technical Support**: Insufficient technical support for troubleshooting and maintaining AI systems.

Impact:

- **Ineffective Use**: Lack of technical expertise can lead to suboptimal use of AI technologies and hinder their benefits.
- **Implementation Challenges**: Difficulty in effectively implementing and managing AI systems due to skill gaps and inadequate training.

5. Interoperability and Integration

Overview: AI solutions often need to work in conjunction with existing agricultural systems and technologies. Interoperability issues can pose challenges in achieving seamless integration.

Challenges:

- **Compatibility**: Difficulty in ensuring that AI systems are compatible with various existing technologies and data formats.
- **System Integration**: Challenges in integrating AI technologies with other farm management systems and tools.
- **Standardization**: Lack of standardized protocols and formats for data and system integration.

Impact:

- **Operational Inefficiencies**: Poor integration can lead to inefficiencies and hinder the effectiveness of AI solutions.
- **Increased Complexity**: Complexity in managing and coordinating multiple systems and technologies.

6. Ethical and Regulatory Concerns

Overview: Ethical and regulatory concerns can affect the development and deployment of AI technologies, impacting their adoption and use in agriculture.

Challenges:

- **Ethical Issues**: Concerns about the ethical implications of using AI, such as data privacy, bias, and fairness.
- **Regulatory Compliance**: Navigating complex regulations related to data protection, AI usage, and technology deployment.
- **Public Perception**: Public skepticism and resistance to AI technologies due to concerns about their impact on jobs and privacy.

Impact:

- **Regulatory Hurdles**: Compliance with regulations can delay the deployment of AI technologies and increase costs.
- **Public Trust**: Ethical concerns and negative public perception can hinder the acceptance and adoption of AI solutions.

Technological barriers pose significant challenges to the widespread adoption and effectiveness of AI-based agricultural solutions. Addressing issues related to data quality, infrastructure, cost, expertise, interoperability, and ethical concerns is crucial for unlocking the full potential of AI in agriculture. By overcoming these barriers, stakeholders can enhance the development, deployment, and impact of AI technologies, driving innovation and improving productivity in the agricultural sector.

Economic and Financial Constraints in AI-Based Agricultural Solutions

Economic and financial constraints are significant barriers to the adoption and effective utilization of AI technologies in agriculture. These constraints can affect various aspects of AI implementation, from initial investments to ongoing operational costs. Here's a detailed look at the key economic and financial challenges:

1. High Initial Investment Costs

Overview: The development and deployment of AI technologies in agriculture often require substantial upfront investment. This includes costs associated with technology acquisition, infrastructure setup, and system integration.

Challenges:

- **Technology Costs**: High costs for advanced AI algorithms, software, and hardware (e.g., sensors, drones, computing resources).
- **Infrastructure Costs**: Expenses related to establishing necessary infrastructure, such as data centers and network connectivity.
- **Integration Costs**: Costs for integrating AI systems with existing agricultural practices and technologies.

Impact:

- **Barrier to Entry**: High initial costs can be prohibitive for smallholder farmers and agricultural businesses, limiting their access to AI technologies.
- **Financial Strain**: Large-scale investments may strain the financial resources of farming enterprises and agricultural organizations.

2. Limited Access to Funding and Financial Support

Overview: Access to funding and financial support is crucial for developing and implementing AI-based agricultural solutions. However, obtaining financial resources can be challenging for many stakeholders.

Challenges:

- **Funding Availability**: Limited availability of grants, loans, and investment opportunities specifically for AI in agriculture.
- **Risk Perception**: Investors may perceive AI in agriculture as a high-risk venture, leading to difficulty in securing funding.
- **Application Complexity**: Complicated application processes for grants and subsidies can deter stakeholders from seeking financial support.

Impact:

- **Delayed Adoption**: Lack of funding can delay the adoption and scaling of AI technologies in agriculture.
- **Innovation Constraints**: Financial constraints may limit research and development efforts, hindering innovation in AI applications.

3. High Operational and Maintenance Costs

Overview: Once AI technologies are implemented, they incur ongoing operational and maintenance costs. These costs can be substantial and affect the sustainability of AI solutions.

Challenges:

- **Maintenance Costs**: Expenses related to maintaining and updating AI systems, including software upgrades and hardware repairs.
- **Operational Costs**: Costs associated with running AI systems, such as data storage, cloud services, and electricity.
- **Technical Support**: Ongoing costs for technical support and troubleshooting, which can be significant for complex AI systems.

Impact:

- **Cost Burden**: High operational and maintenance costs can strain the budgets of farmers and agricultural businesses.
- **Sustainability Issues**: Financial constraints may affect the long-term sustainability and effectiveness of AI solutions.

4. Economic Viability and Return on Investment (ROI)

Overview: Assessing the economic viability and return on investment (ROI) for AI technologies in agriculture is essential for justifying their adoption. However, calculating and ensuring favorable ROI can be challenging.

Challenges:

- **Uncertain ROI**: Difficulty in predicting the financial benefits and returns of AI investments due to varying agricultural conditions and market factors.
- **Cost-Benefit Analysis**: Challenges in performing accurate cost-benefit analyses due to the complexity and novelty of AI technologies.
- **Economic Impact**: Limited empirical data on the economic impact of AI solutions, making it hard to assess their value.

Impact:

- **Investment Hesitation**: Uncertainty regarding ROI may deter stakeholders from investing in AI technologies.
- **Financial Planning**: Difficulty in planning and budgeting for AI investments due to uncertain financial outcomes.

5. Inequities in Resource Distribution

Overview: Economic disparities and inequities in resource distribution can affect the access and adoption of AI technologies across different regions and farmer groups.

Challenges:

- **Regional Disparities**: Differences in economic development and infrastructure between regions can lead to unequal access to AI technologies.
- **Smallholder Farmers**: Smallholder farmers, often in developing regions, may face greater challenges in accessing financial resources and technological support.
- **Economic Inequality**: Economic inequalities can exacerbate the gap between wealthy and less-resourced farmers in adopting AI solutions.

Impact:

- **Unequal Adoption**: Disparities in resource distribution can result in uneven adoption of AI technologies, with more advanced solutions concentrated in wealthier regions.
- **Increased Inequality**: Economic inequities may widen the gap between different farmer groups, affecting overall agricultural development.

6. Market Uncertainties and Economic Fluctuations

Overview: Economic uncertainties and fluctuations in agricultural markets can impact the financial stability and viability of AI investments.

Challenges:

- **Market Volatility**: Fluctuations in commodity prices and market demand can affect the financial returns of AI investments.
- **Economic Downturns**: Economic downturns and financial crises can reduce available funding and investment opportunities for AI technologies.

- **Risk Management**: Difficulty in managing financial risks associated with AI investments due to market uncertainties.

Impact:

- **Investment Risks**: Economic uncertainties can increase the risks associated with investing in AI technologies.
- **Financial Instability**: Market fluctuations can affect the financial stability of agricultural enterprises and their ability to invest in and maintain AI solutions.

Economic and financial constraints pose significant barriers to the adoption and effective use of AI technologies in agriculture. Addressing challenges related to initial investment costs, access to funding, operational expenses, ROI, resource distribution, and market uncertainties is crucial for promoting the widespread implementation of AI solutions. By overcoming these constraints, stakeholders can enhance the financial feasibility and impact of AI technologies, driving innovation and improving agricultural productivity and sustainability.

Lack of Awareness and Education Among Farmers

The effective adoption of AI technologies in agriculture is often hindered by a lack of awareness and education among farmers. This barrier can limit the understanding of AI's benefits, applications, and operational requirements, affecting the overall effectiveness and adoption rates of AI solutions. Here's a detailed look at the issues related to lack of awareness and education:

1. Limited Knowledge of AI Technologies

Overview: Farmers may have limited knowledge about AI technologies, their benefits, and their practical applications in agriculture.

Challenges:

- **Understanding AI Concepts**: Many farmers may not be familiar with basic AI concepts, such as machine learning, data analytics, and automation.
- **Awareness of Applications**: There may be insufficient awareness of how AI technologies can be applied to solve specific agricultural problems, such as crop monitoring, pest control, and yield prediction.

- **Misconceptions**: Misunderstandings and misconceptions about AI may lead to skepticism and reluctance to adopt new technologies.

Impact:

- **Resistance to Adoption**: Lack of knowledge can lead to resistance or reluctance to adopt AI technologies, hindering their potential benefits.
- **Missed Opportunities**: Farmers may miss out on opportunities to improve productivity and efficiency due to limited understanding of available technologies.

2. Insufficient Training and Education Programs

Overview: The availability and accessibility of training and education programs on AI technologies are crucial for empowering farmers with the necessary skills and knowledge.

Challenges:

- **Limited Training Resources**: There may be a shortage of training programs and resources specifically focused on AI technologies in agriculture.
- **Accessibility Issues**: Training programs may not be easily accessible to all farmers, especially those in remote or underserved areas.
- **Lack of Practical Training**: Many training programs may be theoretical and not provide hands-on experience with AI tools and technologies.

Impact:

- **Skill Gaps**: Insufficient training can result in skill gaps, limiting farmers' ability to effectively use and manage AI technologies.
- **Ineffective Implementation**: Without practical training, farmers may struggle to implement AI solutions effectively, leading to suboptimal results.

3. Communication Barriers

Overview: Effective communication between technology providers, educators, and farmers is essential for spreading awareness and education about AI technologies.

Challenges:

- **Language Barriers**: Communication may be hampered by language differences, especially in multilingual regions where technical information is not available in local languages.
- **Technical Jargon**: Use of complex technical jargon and concepts may make it difficult for farmers to understand and engage with AI technologies.
- **Awareness Campaigns**: Limited or ineffective awareness campaigns may fail to reach or resonate with the target audience.

Impact:

- **Ineffective Outreach**: Poor communication can lead to ineffective outreach and education efforts, reducing the impact of awareness programs.
- **Understanding Gaps**: Language and jargon barriers can create gaps in understanding, affecting farmers' ability to make informed decisions about AI technologies.

4. Lack of Demonstration and Pilot Projects

Overview: Demonstration and pilot projects can provide practical insights and hands-on experience with AI technologies, helping farmers understand their benefits and applications.

Challenges:

- **Limited Pilot Projects**: There may be a lack of demonstration farms or pilot projects showcasing the practical use of AI technologies in real-world agricultural settings.
- **Inadequate Showcases**: Existing demonstrations may not adequately showcase the full range of AI applications or may not be tailored to the specific needs of local farmers.

Impact:

- **Limited Adoption**: Without practical demonstrations, farmers may find it difficult to visualize the benefits of AI technologies and be hesitant to adopt them.
- **Uninformed Decisions**: Lack of exposure to pilot projects may lead to uninformed decisions about investing in or implementing AI solutions.

5. Financial Constraints for Training and Education

Overview: Financial constraints can limit the availability and affordability of training and education programs on AI technologies.

Challenges:

- **Training Costs**: The cost of training programs, workshops, and educational materials may be prohibitive for some farmers or agricultural organizations.
- **Funding for Education**: Limited funding for educational initiatives and training programs may restrict their availability and scope.

Impact:

- **Access Issues**: Financial constraints can limit farmers' access to essential training and education, hindering their ability to effectively use AI technologies.
- **Inadequate Skill Development**: Lack of financial resources for training can result in inadequate skill development and reduced effectiveness in implementing AI solutions.

The lack of awareness and education among farmers poses significant barriers to the adoption and effective use of AI technologies in agriculture. Addressing challenges related to knowledge gaps, training availability, communication barriers, demonstration projects, and financial constraints is essential for promoting the successful implementation of AI solutions. By enhancing awareness, providing targeted education, and offering practical training, stakeholders can empower farmers to leverage AI technologies effectively, improving productivity, efficiency, and overall agricultural outcomes.

Infrastructure and Connectivity Issues in AI-Based Agricultural Solutions

Infrastructure and connectivity issues are critical barriers to the effective deployment and utilization of AI technologies in agriculture. These challenges can significantly impact the ability to implement, maintain, and benefit from AI solutions. Here's an in-depth look at the key issues related to infrastructure and connectivity:

1. Internet Connectivity

Overview: Reliable and high-speed internet connectivity is essential for the functioning of AI technologies, especially those that rely on cloud computing, real-time data processing, and remote monitoring.

Challenges:

- **Limited Coverage**: Rural and remote areas often have limited or no access to high-speed internet, affecting the ability to use cloud-based AI services and real-time data transmission.
- **Bandwidth Limitations**: In regions with internet access, bandwidth limitations can affect the performance of AI applications, leading to slow data transfer and processing.
- **Cost of Connectivity**: The cost of high-speed internet can be prohibitive, especially for smallholder farmers and agricultural enterprises.

Impact:

- **Reduced Efficiency**: Poor internet connectivity can reduce the efficiency of AI systems, leading to delays in data processing and analysis.
- **Limited Functionality**: Inadequate connectivity can limit the functionality of AI applications that rely on cloud services and real-time updates.

2. Power Supply Issues

Overview: Consistent and reliable power supply is crucial for operating AI technologies, including sensors, computing devices, and data processing equipment.

Challenges:

- **Power Outages**: Frequent power outages and unstable electricity supply can disrupt the operation of AI systems and data collection processes.
- **Infrastructure Gaps**: Inadequate power infrastructure in rural areas can hinder the installation and operation of AI technologies.
- **Cost of Energy**: High energy costs can be a barrier to the widespread use of power-intensive AI technologies.

Impact:

- **Operational Disruptions**: Power supply issues can lead to interruptions in AI system operations, affecting data collection and analysis.
- **Increased Costs**: Higher energy costs can increase the overall cost of using AI technologies, impacting financial feasibility.

3. Technological Infrastructure

Overview: The successful implementation of AI technologies requires robust technological infrastructure, including data centers, computing resources, and storage solutions.

Challenges:

- **Lack of Data Centers**: Inadequate data centers in rural areas can affect the ability to process and store large volumes of agricultural data.
- **Limited Computing Resources**: Insufficient access to high-performance computing resources can limit the development and deployment of advanced AI models.
- **Storage Constraints**: Limited storage capacity for handling and analyzing large datasets can hinder the effectiveness of AI solutions.

Impact:

- **Data Management Issues**: Poor technological infrastructure can lead to challenges in managing and processing agricultural data effectively.
- **Development Constraints**: Lack of infrastructure can constrain the development and deployment of advanced AI technologies.

4. Infrastructure for Sensor Deployment

Overview: AI applications in agriculture often rely on various sensors (e.g., weather sensors, soil moisture sensors) to collect real-time data. Effective deployment of these sensors requires appropriate infrastructure.

Challenges:

- **Installation Difficulties**: Lack of infrastructure for installing and maintaining sensors in remote or rural areas can limit data collection capabilities.
- **Maintenance Challenges**: Difficulty in accessing and maintaining sensors in areas with poor infrastructure can affect their reliability and performance.

- **Integration Issues**: Challenges in integrating sensor data with AI systems due to infrastructure constraints can hinder the effectiveness of AI solutions.

Impact:

- **Inaccurate Data**: Poor sensor deployment and maintenance can lead to inaccurate or incomplete data, affecting the performance of AI models.
- **Reduced Effectiveness**: Limited sensor infrastructure can reduce the overall effectiveness of AI applications that rely on real-time data.

5. Accessibility and Affordability of Technology

Overview: The accessibility and affordability of technology are crucial for the widespread adoption of AI solutions in agriculture.

Challenges:

- **High Costs**: The cost of technology infrastructure, including hardware, software, and connectivity, can be prohibitive for many farmers and agricultural enterprises.
- **Limited Availability**: Access to advanced technological infrastructure may be limited in certain regions, affecting the ability to deploy AI solutions.
- **Economic Disparities**: Economic disparities can affect the ability of different regions and farmer groups to invest in and maintain the necessary technology infrastructure.

Impact:

- **Limited Adoption**: High costs and limited availability of technology can hinder the adoption of AI solutions, especially among smallholder farmers and less-resourced regions.
- **Economic Inequality**: Disparities in technology access can exacerbate economic inequalities between different farming communities.

6. Data Security and Privacy

Overview: Ensuring data security and privacy is essential for protecting sensitive agricultural data and maintaining trust in AI technologies.

Challenges:

- **Security Risks**: Inadequate infrastructure for securing data can expose agricultural data to risks such as cyberattacks and unauthorized access.
- **Compliance Issues**: Compliance with data protection regulations and standards can be challenging in areas with limited technological infrastructure.
- **Data Integrity**: Ensuring the integrity and accuracy of data collected and processed by AI systems is crucial for reliable results.

Impact:

- **Data Breaches**: Poor data security can lead to breaches, affecting the confidentiality and integrity of agricultural data.
- **Regulatory Challenges**: Compliance with data protection regulations can be challenging, affecting the deployment and use of AI technologies.

Infrastructure and connectivity issues pose significant barriers to the effective deployment and utilization of AI technologies in agriculture. Addressing challenges related to internet connectivity, power supply, technological infrastructure, sensor deployment, technology accessibility, and data security is crucial for promoting the successful implementation of AI solutions. By improving infrastructure and connectivity, stakeholders can enhance the feasibility and impact of AI technologies, driving innovation and improving agricultural productivity and sustainability.

Ethical and Environmental Considerations in AI-Based Agricultural Solutions

The integration of AI technologies into agriculture brings significant benefits, but it also raises important ethical and environmental considerations. Addressing these concerns is crucial for ensuring that AI applications contribute to sustainable and equitable agricultural practices. Here's an in-depth exploration of the key ethical and environmental considerations:

1. Data Privacy and Security

Overview: AI systems in agriculture often rely on large amounts of data, including personal and sensitive information about farmers and agricultural practices.

Ethical Considerations:

- **Data Privacy**: Ensuring that farmers' personal data and proprietary agricultural information are protected from unauthorized access and misuse.
- **Consent**: Obtaining informed consent from farmers for the collection and use of their data.
- **Data Ownership**: Clarifying who owns the data collected and how it can be used by various stakeholders.

Impact:

- **Trust Issues**: Privacy breaches or misuse of data can erode trust in AI technologies and their providers.
- **Legal and Regulatory Compliance**: Ensuring compliance with data protection regulations is essential to avoid legal repercussions and maintain ethical standards.

2. Bias and Fairness

Overview: AI algorithms can sometimes reflect and perpetuate biases present in the data they are trained on, leading to unfair or discriminatory outcomes.

Ethical Considerations:

- **Bias in Data**: Addressing biases in agricultural data that may lead to unfair treatment of certain groups of farmers or regions.
- **Equitable Access**: Ensuring that AI technologies benefit all farmers equally, regardless of their socio-economic status or geographic location.
- **Transparency**: Making AI algorithms and decision-making processes transparent to stakeholders to ensure fairness.

Impact:

- **Inequality**: Bias in AI systems can exacerbate existing inequalities and disadvantage marginalized or less-resourced farming communities.
- **Credibility**: Lack of fairness and transparency can undermine the credibility and effectiveness of AI solutions.

3. Environmental Impact

Overview: AI technologies can have various environmental impacts, both positive and negative, depending on their implementation and usage.

Environmental Considerations:

- **Resource Use**: Assessing the environmental impact of the resources required for developing, deploying, and operating AI technologies, such as energy consumption and electronic waste.
- **Sustainable Practices**: Ensuring that AI applications promote sustainable agricultural practices and contribute to environmental conservation.
- **Monitoring and Management**: Using AI to monitor and manage environmental impacts, such as soil health, water use, and biodiversity.

Impact:

- **Resource Depletion**: High energy consumption and resource use associated with AI technologies can contribute to environmental degradation.
- **Sustainability**: AI applications that promote sustainable practices can help mitigate negative environmental impacts and support conservation efforts.

4. Impact on Employment

Overview: The adoption of AI technologies in agriculture may affect employment patterns, with potential implications for farm labor and rural economies.

Ethical Considerations:

- **Job Displacement**: Addressing concerns about job displacement due to automation and the reduction of labor-intensive tasks.
- **Skill Development**: Providing training and support for workers to adapt to new roles and skills required by AI technologies.
- **Economic Impact**: Assessing the broader economic impact on rural communities and ensuring that AI adoption benefits local economies.

Impact:

- **Employment Shifts**: AI technologies may shift job roles and create new opportunities, but also may lead to job loss in certain sectors.
- **Economic Inequality**: The displacement of workers without adequate support can exacerbate economic inequalities in rural areas.

5. Ethical Use of AI

Overview: The ethical use of AI involves ensuring that AI technologies are developed and used in ways that align with ethical principles and societal values.

Ethical Considerations:

- **Responsible Innovation**: Ensuring that AI technologies are developed with ethical considerations in mind, including potential risks and unintended consequences.
- **Accountability**: Holding developers and users accountable for the ethical use of AI technologies, including addressing any adverse effects.
- **Beneficence**: Designing AI applications that aim to benefit society as a whole and improve the well-being of farmers and communities.

Impact:

- **Ethical Dilemmas**: The ethical use of AI requires addressing complex dilemmas related to technology deployment and ensuring alignment with societal values.
- **Public Trust**: Ethical practices in AI development and use can enhance public trust and acceptance of AI technologies.

6. Socio-Cultural Implications

Overview: AI technologies can have socio-cultural implications, influencing agricultural practices, community dynamics, and cultural values.

Ethical Considerations:

- **Cultural Sensitivity**: Ensuring that AI technologies respect and align with local cultural practices and values.
- **Community Impact**: Assessing how AI solutions impact community dynamics, social structures, and traditional practices.

- **Inclusivity**: Ensuring that AI technologies are inclusive and consider the diverse needs and perspectives of different communities.

Impact:

- **Cultural Displacement**: AI technologies may disrupt traditional practices and cultural values, affecting community cohesion and identity.
- **Social Integration**: Inclusive and culturally sensitive AI solutions can enhance social integration and support community well-being.

Ethical and environmental considerations are crucial for the responsible implementation of AI technologies in agriculture. Addressing issues related to data privacy, bias, environmental impact, employment, ethical use, and socio-cultural implications is essential for ensuring that AI applications contribute to sustainable and equitable agricultural practices. By prioritizing these considerations, stakeholders can promote the positive impact of AI technologies while mitigating potential risks and challenges.

CHAPTER VII

Future Prospects and Innovations in AI for Indian Agriculture

Emerging AI Technologies and Trends in Agriculture

The field of artificial intelligence (AI) is rapidly evolving, bringing new technologies and trends that are transforming agriculture. These emerging technologies offer innovative solutions to enhance productivity, sustainability, and efficiency in farming. Here's an overview of some of the key emerging AI technologies and trends in agriculture:

Advanced Machine Learning Models

Machine learning models are becoming increasingly sophisticated, enabling more accurate predictions and insights from agricultural data. Trends include deep learning, which uses algorithms for complex tasks like image recognition and disease detection; transfer learning, which applies pre-trained models to new problems; and explainable AI (XAI), which provides transparent explanations for predictions and decisions. These advancements improve accuracy in crop yield predictions, disease outbreaks, and weather impacts, enhancing operational efficiency through effective analysis of large datasets.

AI-Driven Robotics

Robotics integrated with AI is revolutionizing various aspects of farming, from planting and harvesting to maintenance and monitoring. Trends include autonomous tractors for precision planting and harvesting, drones equipped with AI for aerial surveillance and targeted application of inputs, and robotic harvesters designed for fruit and vegetable harvesting. These technologies reduce manual labor, increase efficiency, and enhance precision in various farming tasks, leading to better crop yields and reduced waste.

Smart Sensors and IoT Integration

The integration of AI with smart sensors and the Internet of Things (IoT) provides real-time monitoring and data collection capabilities. Trends include soil sensors that measure moisture, temperature, and nutrient levels, weather stations enhanced with AI for accurate forecasts, and IoT networks that offer comprehensive data collection and management. This real-time data allows for better resource management and improved decision-making, based on accurate and timely information.

Precision Agriculture with AI

AI-driven precision agriculture focuses on optimizing farming practices by using data to make precise decisions. Trends include variable rate technology (VRT) that adjusts input application rates based on field variability, precision irrigation systems that optimize water usage, and site-specific management that tailors practices to specific field areas. These innovations lead to more efficient use of resources such as water, fertilizers, and pesticides, resulting in cost savings and reduced environmental impact, while also improving crop yields.

AI in Genomic and Breeding Research

AI is increasingly used in genomic research and crop breeding to accelerate the development of new varieties. Trends include genomic selection, where AI analyzes genetic data to predict performance, trait prediction for optimizing breeding strategies, and high-throughput phenotyping for analyzing large-scale data to select superior plants. These advancements speed up the development of improved crop varieties and enhance understanding of genetic factors affecting crop performance and resilience.

AI-Enhanced Supply Chain Management

AI technologies are improving supply chain management in agriculture by optimizing logistics, reducing waste, and enhancing transparency. Trends include predictive analytics for forecasting demand and managing inventory, blockchain integration for traceability and transparency, and demand forecasting to adjust production and distribution. These technologies reduce food waste, improve efficiency, and enhance the quality of agricultural products through better supply chain management.

AI in Sustainable Farming Practices

AI technologies support the adoption of sustainable farming practices by optimizing resource use and reducing environmental impact. Trends include carbon footprint reduction through monitoring and managing greenhouse gas emissions, sustainable resource management for optimizing water and energy use, and biodiversity monitoring to promote ecological balance. These advancements contribute to environmental sustainability by reducing waste and promoting conservation practices in agriculture.

Emerging AI technologies and trends are driving significant advancements in agriculture, offering innovative solutions to enhance productivity, efficiency, and sustainability. From advanced machine learning models and AI-driven robotics to smart sensors and sustainable farming practices, these technologies are shaping the future of agriculture. Embracing these trends allows stakeholders to address current challenges and unlock new opportunities for growth and innovation in the agricultural sector.

Potential Impact of AI on Productivity and Sustainability in Agriculture

AI technologies are poised to revolutionize agriculture by significantly enhancing productivity and promoting sustainability. Here's a detailed look at how AI can impact these critical aspects:

Enhancing Productivity

AI technologies contribute to increased agricultural productivity through several key mechanisms:

- **Precision Agriculture**: AI-driven precision agriculture enables more accurate and efficient farming practices. By using data from sensors, drones, and satellite imagery, AI can optimize planting patterns, irrigation schedules, and nutrient applications. This leads to better crop yields and more efficient use of resources.
- **Yield Prediction and Forecasting**: AI models analyze historical data, weather patterns, and crop performance to predict future yields. Accurate yield forecasts help farmers make informed decisions about resource allocation, crop management, and market strategies, ultimately improving overall productivity.
- **Robotics and Automation**: AI-powered robots and autonomous machines perform repetitive and labor-intensive tasks such as planting, weeding, and harvesting with high precision and speed. This reduces the reliance on manual labor, increases operational efficiency, and allows for more timely interventions.
- **Pest and Disease Management**: AI systems use image recognition and pattern analysis to detect pests and diseases early. Early detection enables targeted treatments, reducing crop losses and improving overall productivity by preventing the spread of diseases and pests.
- **Resource Optimization**: AI optimizes the use of resources such as water, fertilizers, and pesticides by analyzing real-time data from various sources. This reduces waste and ensures that inputs are applied where and when they are needed most, enhancing crop growth and

productivity.

Promoting Sustainability

AI also plays a crucial role in promoting sustainable agricultural practices:

- **Environmental Conservation**: AI technologies help monitor and manage environmental factors such as soil health, water usage, and biodiversity. By analyzing data on soil conditions and crop performance, AI can recommend practices that conserve resources and minimize environmental impact.
- **Reduced Chemical Usage**: AI systems optimize the application of fertilizers and pesticides, reducing the overall quantity used. This minimizes runoff and pollution, leading to healthier ecosystems and less environmental degradation.
- **Water Management**: AI-powered irrigation systems use data from soil moisture sensors and weather forecasts to optimize water use. This reduces water waste and promotes efficient irrigation practices, crucial in areas facing water scarcity.
- **Carbon Footprint Reduction**: AI helps in tracking and managing greenhouse gas emissions from agricultural practices. By optimizing processes and reducing the use of inputs, AI can contribute to lowering the carbon footprint of farming operations.
- **Sustainable Breeding Practices**: AI accelerates the development of crop varieties that are more resilient to environmental stresses and diseases. This promotes sustainability by reducing the need for chemical inputs and improving the adaptability of crops to changing climate conditions.
- **Waste Reduction**: AI technologies improve supply chain management by optimizing logistics, reducing food waste, and enhancing traceability. This ensures that products reach the market efficiently and reduces the amount of food lost throughout the supply chain.

AI technologies have the potential to significantly enhance agricultural productivity and promote sustainability. By leveraging precision agriculture, robotics, and advanced data analytics, AI can optimize farming practices, improve resource management, and support environmental conservation. The integration of AI in agriculture not only boosts productivity but also contributes to more sustainable and environmentally-friendly farming practices, paving the way for a more resilient and efficient agricultural sector.

AI for Climate-Resilient Agriculture

AI technologies are increasingly being utilized to develop climate-resilient agricultural practices that can adapt to and mitigate the effects of climate change. Here's how AI contributes to creating more resilient agricultural systems:

1. Climate Data Analysis and Forecasting

AI enhances the analysis of climate data and forecasting, which is crucial for adapting agricultural practices to changing weather patterns.

- **Advanced Climate Models**: AI algorithms analyze vast amounts of historical and real-time climate data to improve predictions of climate patterns and extreme weather events. These models help farmers anticipate changes and prepare for potential impacts on their crops and livestock.
- **Localized Weather Forecasting**: AI provides highly localized weather forecasts using data from various sources, including satellites and weather stations. Accurate, localized forecasts enable farmers to make timely decisions about planting, harvesting, and managing their crops.

2. Crop Selection and Breeding

AI supports the development of crop varieties that are more resilient to climate stresses such as drought, heat, and flooding.

- **Genomic Analysis**: AI-driven genomic tools analyze the genetic makeup of crops to identify traits associated with resilience to environmental stresses. This accelerates the breeding of climate-resistant crop varieties.
- **Trait Prediction**: AI models predict how different crop varieties will perform under various climate conditions, helping breeders select the most suitable varieties for specific environments.

3. Precision Agriculture for Stress Management

AI technologies optimize agricultural practices to manage and mitigate the impacts of climate-induced stresses on crops.

- **Optimized Irrigation**: AI systems use data from soil moisture sensors, weather forecasts, and crop needs to design precise irrigation schedules, reducing water waste and improving drought resilience.

- **Nutrient Management**: AI analyzes soil conditions and crop health to optimize the application of fertilizers and nutrients. This helps crops cope with environmental stresses and maintain productivity.
- **Pest and Disease Management**: AI helps in early detection and management of pests and diseases, which can be exacerbated by climate change. Early intervention minimizes crop losses and enhances resilience.

4. Soil Health and Conservation

AI plays a key role in monitoring and improving soil health, which is vital for maintaining agricultural productivity in the face of climate change.

- **Soil Monitoring**: AI-driven sensors and analytics track soil health indicators such as moisture levels, nutrient content, and microbial activity. This information guides soil management practices that enhance soil resilience and fertility.
- **Erosion Control**: AI models predict soil erosion patterns and recommend conservation practices to prevent soil loss and degradation, which can be intensified by extreme weather events.

5. Sustainable Water Management

Effective water management is critical for adapting to climate variability, and AI provides tools for optimizing water use.

- **Smart Irrigation Systems**: AI-powered irrigation systems adjust water application based on real-time data from soil sensors, weather forecasts, and crop needs. This ensures efficient water use and enhances drought resilience.
- **Water Resource Planning**: AI models help in planning and managing water resources by predicting water availability and demand, which is crucial for adapting to changes in precipitation patterns.

6. Risk Assessment and Decision Support

AI assists in assessing risks and providing decision support for managing climate-related challenges.

- **Risk Modeling**: AI algorithms evaluate the risk of climate-related events such as floods, droughts, and heatwaves. This helps farmers prepare for and mitigate the impacts of these events on their operations.
- **Decision Support Systems**: AI-driven decision support systems provide actionable insights and recommendations for adapting agricultural practices to changing climate conditions. These systems help farmers make informed decisions to enhance resilience and productivity.

7. Community and Policy Support

AI also supports broader efforts to build climate resilience through community engagement and policy development.

- **Farmer Education and Training**: AI-powered platforms provide farmers with training and information on climate-resilient practices, helping them adapt to changing conditions.
- **Policy Development**: AI helps policymakers analyze data and develop strategies to support climate-resilient agriculture. This includes creating policies for resource management, disaster response, and sustainable farming practices.

AI technologies are crucial in developing climate-resilient agriculture by improving climate data analysis, supporting crop breeding, optimizing agricultural practices, and enhancing water and soil management. By leveraging AI, farmers and policymakers can better adapt to the challenges posed by climate change, ensuring sustainable and productive agricultural systems. AI's role in climate resilience is instrumental in safeguarding food security and promoting environmental sustainability in the face of a changing climate.

The Role of AI in Organic and Sustainable Farming

AI is increasingly becoming a valuable tool in organic and sustainable farming, offering innovative solutions that align with the principles of environmental stewardship, resource efficiency, and reduced chemical use. Here's how AI is contributing to these farming practices:

1. Precision Agriculture

AI enhances precision agriculture techniques that are central to sustainable farming by optimizing the use of resources and minimizing waste.

- **Targeted Inputs**: AI systems analyze data from sensors and satellite imagery to apply inputs such as water, fertilizers, and pesticides only where and when they are needed. This reduces the overall quantity of inputs used and minimizes environmental impact, aligning with organic principles.
- **Variable Rate Technology (VRT)**: AI-driven VRT adjusts application rates of inputs based on real-time data, improving efficiency and reducing the risk of over-application. This helps maintain soil health and reduces the ecological footprint of farming.

2. Soil Health Monitoring

Maintaining soil health is crucial in organic farming, and AI offers advanced tools for monitoring and managing soil conditions.

- **Soil Sensors**: AI-powered soil sensors measure parameters such as moisture, pH, and nutrient levels. This data helps in making informed decisions about soil management practices, ensuring that soil remains fertile and balanced.
- **Soil Health Analytics**: AI models analyze data from soil sensors to provide insights into soil health trends and recommend practices to enhance soil quality, such as crop rotation and organic amendments.

3. Pest and Disease Management

AI supports sustainable pest and disease management by reducing the reliance on chemical pesticides and promoting integrated pest management (IPM) strategies.

- **Early Detection**: AI-driven image recognition and pattern analysis identify pests and diseases at early stages. Early detection allows for targeted interventions, reducing the need for broad-spectrum chemical treatments.
- **Predictive Analytics**: AI models predict pest and disease outbreaks based on historical data and environmental conditions, enabling proactive measures and reducing reliance on chemicals.

4. Sustainable Water Management

Efficient water use is essential for sustainability, and AI provides tools to optimize irrigation and manage water resources.

- **Smart Irrigation Systems**: AI systems use data from soil moisture sensors, weather forecasts, and crop needs to optimize irrigation schedules. This reduces water waste and supports sustainable water use practices.
- **Water Resource Planning**: AI models help in planning and managing water resources by predicting water availability and demand, ensuring that water use is both efficient and sustainable.

5. Organic Crop Management

AI contributes to the management of organic crops by enhancing monitoring and decision-making processes.

- **Crop Monitoring**: AI-powered tools monitor crop health and growth using data from drones and sensors. This helps in identifying and addressing issues without the use of synthetic chemicals, in line with organic farming standards.
- **Nutrient Management**: AI analyzes soil and plant data to recommend organic nutrient sources and management practices. This ensures that crops receive adequate nutrition while adhering to organic principles.

6. Waste Reduction and Recycling

AI technologies support waste reduction and recycling practices in organic farming, contributing to sustainability.

- **Composting Optimization**: AI models analyze composting processes to optimize conditions such as temperature and moisture, improving the efficiency of organic waste recycling.
- **Resource Recovery**: AI helps in identifying opportunities for resource recovery and recycling within the farming system, reducing waste and promoting circular agricultural practices.

7. Data-Driven Decision Making

AI enables data-driven decision-making, which is crucial for managing organic and sustainable farming practices effectively.

- **Decision Support Systems**: AI-driven decision support systems provide actionable insights based on data from various sources, including weather forecasts, soil sensors, and crop performance metrics. This helps farmers make informed decisions that align with organic and sustainability goals.

- **Farm Management Platforms**: AI-powered farm management platforms integrate data from different sources to provide a holistic view of farm operations, enabling farmers to optimize practices and maintain sustainability.

8. Research and Innovation

AI supports research and innovation in organic farming by accelerating the development of new practices and technologies.

- **Crop Breeding**: AI accelerates the development of organic-compatible crop varieties by analyzing genetic data and performance metrics. This helps in breeding crops that are better suited to organic farming systems.
- **Sustainable Practices Research**: AI assists researchers in analyzing the effectiveness of various sustainable practices and developing new strategies for improving organic farming systems.

AI plays a transformative role in organic and sustainable farming by enhancing precision agriculture, improving soil health, managing pests and diseases, optimizing water use, and supporting organic crop management. By leveraging AI technologies, farmers can achieve greater efficiency, reduce environmental impact, and adhere to organic principles, contributing to a more sustainable and resilient agricultural system. AI's integration into organic and sustainable farming practices supports the goals of reducing chemical inputs, conserving resources, and promoting environmental stewardship.

AI in Agricultural Research and Development

Artificial Intelligence (AI) is playing an increasingly pivotal role in agricultural research and development (R&D). By enhancing data analysis, accelerating discovery, and optimizing experimental processes, AI is driving innovations that address global agricultural challenges and improve farming practices. Here's how AI is shaping agricultural R&D:

1. Accelerating Crop Breeding

AI accelerates the crop breeding process by analyzing large datasets and identifying desirable traits more efficiently.

- **Genomic Data Analysis**: AI algorithms analyze genomic data to identify genes associated with important traits such as disease resistance, drought tolerance, and yield. This speeds up the development of new crop varieties with enhanced characteristics.
- **Predictive Breeding**: AI models predict the outcomes of breeding experiments based on genetic information and environmental factors. This helps breeders select the most promising candidates for further development, reducing time and costs.

2. Enhancing Phenotyping

Phenotyping involves measuring plant traits and characteristics, and AI enhances this process through advanced imaging and data analysis.

- **Automated Imaging**: AI-powered imaging systems capture detailed images of plants and analyze them to assess traits such as growth, leaf area, and flowering. This provides high-throughput phenotyping capabilities and improves the accuracy of trait assessments.
- **Trait Prediction**: AI models analyze phenotypic data to predict how plants will perform under various conditions. This helps researchers identify traits that are crucial for adaptation and productivity.

3. Optimizing Experimental Design

AI optimizes the design and execution of agricultural experiments, improving the efficiency and effectiveness of research.

- **Experimental Design**: AI algorithms assist in designing experiments by selecting optimal conditions and parameters based on previous research and data analysis. This helps in conducting more efficient and informative experiments.
- **Data Integration**: AI integrates data from various sources, including field trials, lab experiments, and remote sensing, to provide a comprehensive view of research outcomes. This facilitates better decision-making and more accurate conclusions.

4. Disease and Pest Management

AI contributes to research on disease and pest management by providing tools for early detection and control strategies.

- **Disease Diagnostics**: AI-powered image recognition systems identify plant diseases and pests from images of leaves and stems. This enables early diagnosis and targeted treatment strategies.
- **Predictive Models**: AI models predict the spread of diseases and pest infestations based on environmental conditions and historical data. This helps researchers develop proactive management strategies.

5. Soil and Environmental Research

AI supports research on soil health and environmental factors that affect agricultural productivity.

- **Soil Analysis**: AI algorithms analyze soil data from sensors and laboratory tests to assess soil health and recommend management practices. This helps in understanding soil variability and improving crop performance.
- **Environmental Impact Assessment**: AI models evaluate the impact of various agricultural practices on the environment, including factors such as greenhouse gas emissions, water usage, and biodiversity.

6. Climate Change Adaptation

AI plays a crucial role in researching and developing strategies for adapting agriculture to climate change.

- **Climate Models**: AI-enhanced climate models predict the effects of climate change on crop growth and yield. This helps in developing adaptation strategies and selecting climate-resilient crop varieties.
- **Adaptation Strategies**: AI analyzes data on climate variables and crop performance to develop and optimize adaptation strategies, such as changes in planting dates, crop varieties, and management practices.

7. Data-Driven Insights

AI provides data-driven insights that guide agricultural research and innovation.

- **Big Data Analysis**: AI analyzes large datasets from various sources, including satellite imagery, weather data, and field observations, to uncover patterns and trends that inform research.

- **Decision Support**: AI-driven decision support systems offer recommendations and insights based on data analysis, helping researchers make informed decisions and prioritize research activities.

8. Enhancing Collaboration and Knowledge Sharing

AI facilitates collaboration and knowledge sharing among researchers and stakeholders.

- **Collaborative Platforms**: AI-powered platforms enable researchers to share data, insights, and findings, fostering collaboration and accelerating the pace of discovery.
- **Knowledge Extraction**: AI systems extract relevant information from scientific literature and research publications, helping researchers stay updated with the latest advancements and integrate new knowledge into their work.

AI is transforming agricultural research and development by accelerating crop breeding, enhancing phenotyping, optimizing experimental design, and supporting disease and pest management. It also aids in soil and environmental research, climate change adaptation, and data-driven insights. By integrating AI technologies, researchers can achieve more efficient, effective, and innovative solutions to address the complex challenges facing agriculture and drive advancements in the field. AI's role in agricultural R&D is pivotal in enhancing productivity, sustainability, and resilience in the global food system.

CHAPTER VIII

Policy Framework and Government Support

Current Policies Supporting AI in Agriculture

1. National Agricultural Policy

Many countries have national agricultural policies that emphasize the adoption of technology, including AI, to boost agricultural productivity and sustainability. These policies often include:

- **Investment in Research and Development (R&D)**: Governments allocate funds to support agricultural R&D, including projects that focus on AI applications in farming.
- **Technology Adoption Programs**: Policies that promote the adoption of modern technologies, including AI, through subsidies, grants, or loans for farmers and agribusinesses.

2. Digital Agriculture Initiatives

Governments are increasingly focusing on digital agriculture initiatives to leverage AI for improving agricultural practices.

- **Digital India Program**: In India, the Digital India program aims to enhance digital infrastructure and promote the use of technology, including AI, in various sectors, including agriculture.
- **Smart Agriculture Schemes**: Various schemes support the deployment of smart agriculture technologies, including AI-driven tools for precision farming, pest management, and crop monitoring.

3. Agricultural Innovation Funds

Governments are establishing innovation funds to support the development and deployment of AI technologies in agriculture.

- **Innovation Grants**: Grants and funding opportunities for startups and research institutions working on AI solutions for agriculture.
- **Seed Funding**: Financial support for early-stage projects and pilot programs that test AI applications in real-world agricultural settings.

4. Data Privacy and Security Regulations

Policies related to data privacy and security are crucial for the effective use of AI in agriculture.

- **Data Protection Laws**: Regulations that ensure the secure handling of data collected through AI systems, protecting farmers' and consumers' privacy.
- **Data Sharing Agreements**: Policies that facilitate data sharing among researchers, farmers, and agribusinesses while maintaining data security and confidentiality.

5. Education and Training Programs

To ensure effective AI adoption, policies often include education and training initiatives.

- **Skill Development Programs**: Training programs for farmers and agricultural professionals to build skills in using AI technologies and interpreting AI-generated data.
- **Educational Partnerships**: Collaborations between educational institutions and industry to integrate AI and data science into agricultural curricula.

Future Policy Recommendations
1. Comprehensive AI Strategy for Agriculture

- **National AI Strategy**: Develop a comprehensive national AI strategy for agriculture that outlines clear goals, funding priorities, and action plans for integrating AI into farming practices.
- **Long-Term Vision**: Establish a long-term vision for AI in agriculture, including targets for AI adoption, innovation, and sustainability.

2. Enhanced Funding and Incentives

- **Increased R&D Funding**: Increase funding for agricultural R&D focused on AI technologies to drive innovation and support the development of new solutions.
- **Incentives for Adoption**: Provide additional incentives for farmers and agribusinesses to adopt AI technologies, such as tax breaks, subsidies, or

low-interest loans.

3. Improved Data Governance

- **Data Sharing Frameworks**: Develop frameworks for secure and transparent data sharing among stakeholders, including farmers, researchers, and policymakers.
- **Data Standards and Interoperability**: Establish standards for data collection, management, and interoperability to facilitate the integration of AI systems across different platforms.

4. Support for Smallholder Farmers

- **Affordable AI Solutions**: Promote the development and dissemination of affordable AI solutions tailored to the needs of smallholder farmers.
- **Training and Support**: Enhance training programs and support services to help smallholder farmers effectively use AI technologies and benefit from their applications.

5. Strengthening Public-Private Partnerships

- **Collaborative Projects**: Encourage collaborative projects between public institutions, private companies, and research organizations to advance AI in agriculture.
- **Innovation Hubs**: Establish innovation hubs and incubators that bring together stakeholders to develop and test new AI technologies and solutions.

Role of Government and Private Sector Collaboration
1. Joint Research and Development

- **Collaborative R&D**: Governments and private companies can collaborate on R&D projects to develop new AI technologies for agriculture, sharing resources, expertise, and funding.
- **Public-Private Partnerships (PPPs)**: PPPs can accelerate the deployment of AI solutions by combining public funding with private sector innovation and efficiency.

2. Infrastructure Development

- **Shared Infrastructure**: Collaboration on building and maintaining digital infrastructure, such as data centers and high-speed internet, to support AI applications in agriculture.
- **Resource Sharing**: Private companies can contribute technical expertise and infrastructure, while governments provide regulatory support and funding.

3. Policy and Regulation

- **Regulatory Frameworks**: Develop joint regulatory frameworks that balance innovation with data privacy and security concerns, ensuring the responsible use of AI technologies.
- **Standards Development**: Collaborate on developing industry standards for AI technologies in agriculture to ensure interoperability and quality.

4. Training and Capacity Building

- **Training Programs**: Develop joint training programs to build the skills of agricultural professionals and farmers in using AI technologies effectively.
- **Knowledge Sharing**: Share best practices, case studies, and success stories to facilitate the adoption of AI solutions across different regions and sectors.

International Cooperation and Knowledge Sharing
1. Global Research Collaborations

- **International Research Projects**: Participate in international research collaborations to advance AI technologies and share knowledge on best practices and innovations.
- **Global Conferences and Workshops**: Engage in global conferences and workshops focused on AI in agriculture to exchange ideas, research findings, and technological advancements.

2. Knowledge Exchange Platforms

- **Global Platforms**: Establish global platforms for knowledge exchange and collaboration, where researchers, policymakers, and industry leaders can share insights and developments.
- **Best Practices**: Document and disseminate best practices and successful case studies from different countries to promote effective use of AI in agriculture worldwide.

3. Cross-Border Partnerships

- **Bilateral and Multilateral Agreements**: Form bilateral and multilateral agreements to support AI research, technology transfer, and collaborative projects in agriculture.
- **Capacity Building**: Support capacity-building initiatives in developing countries to help them adopt and benefit from AI technologies in agriculture.

4. International Standards and Regulations

- **Global Standards**: Work towards the development of international standards and regulations for AI technologies in agriculture to ensure consistency and interoperability.
- **Regulatory Harmonization**: Collaborate on harmonizing regulations and policies to facilitate cross-border technology transfer and innovation.

AI's integration into agriculture is supported by a range of current policies, with future recommendations focusing on enhanced funding, improved data governance, and support for smallholder farmers. Government and private sector collaboration is crucial for advancing AI technologies, while international cooperation fosters global knowledge sharing and innovation. Together, these efforts can drive the development and deployment of AI solutions that improve agricultural productivity, sustainability, and resilience.

CHAPTER IX

The Economic Impact of AI on Indian Agriculture

Cost-Benefit Analysis of AI Adoption in Agriculture

A comprehensive cost-benefit analysis of AI adoption in agriculture helps in understanding the economic implications, potential gains, and challenges associated with integrating AI technologies into farming practices. This analysis covers various aspects such as implementation costs, potential benefits, and the overall impact on agricultural productivity and sustainability.

Costs of AI Adoption

Initial Investment

- Technology Acquisition: Costs associated with purchasing AI-powered tools and systems, such as sensors, drones, and software.
- Infrastructure Setup: Expenses for establishing necessary infrastructure, including data storage solutions, high-speed internet, and computing resources.

Development and Customization

- Software Development: Costs related to developing or customizing AI algorithms and software tailored to specific agricultural needs.
- Integration: Expenses for integrating AI systems with existing farm management practices and technologies.

Training and Capacity Building

- Farmer Training: Costs for training farmers and agricultural professionals to effectively use AI technologies and interpret AI-generated data.
- Technical Support: Ongoing costs for technical support and maintenance of AI systems.

Data Management

- Data Collection: Expenses related to collecting and managing large volumes of data required for AI analysis.
- Data Security: Costs for ensuring data security and compliance with privacy regulations.

Benefits of AI Adoption
Increased Productivity

- Yield Improvement: AI-driven precision farming techniques, such as optimized irrigation and nutrient management, can lead to significant improvements in crop yield and quality.
- Resource Efficiency: AI helps in the efficient use of resources, such as water, fertilizers, and pesticides, reducing waste and increasing overall productivity.

Cost Savings

- Operational Efficiency: Automation of repetitive tasks and optimization of farm operations can reduce labor costs and operational expenses.
- Reduced Input Costs: AI technologies help in minimizing the use of inputs like fertilizers and pesticides, leading to lower input costs.

Enhanced Decision-Making

- Data-Driven Insights: AI provides actionable insights based on data analysis, improving decision-making related to crop management, pest control, and market strategies.
- Predictive Analytics: AI models predict crop yields, weather conditions, and pest outbreaks, allowing for better planning and risk management.

Risk Management

- Early Detection: AI systems can detect diseases, pests, and other issues early, enabling timely interventions and reducing crop losses.
- Climate Adaptation: AI helps in developing strategies for adapting to climate change, such as selecting suitable crop varieties and optimizing

planting schedules.

Environmental Benefits

- Sustainable Practices: AI promotes sustainable agricultural practices by optimizing resource use and reducing the environmental impact of farming activities.
- Reduced Emissions: Efficient use of resources and reduced chemical inputs contribute to lower greenhouse gas emissions and improved environmental health.

Challenges and Considerations
Implementation Challenges

- High Initial Costs: The high initial investment required for AI technologies can be a barrier, especially for smallholder farmers.
- Technical Complexity: The complexity of AI systems may pose challenges in terms of implementation and operation, requiring specialized knowledge and skills.

Data and Privacy Concerns

- Data Management: Handling and securing large volumes of data can be challenging and costly.
- Privacy Issues: Ensuring data privacy and compliance with regulations is crucial to protect sensitive information.

Adoption Barriers

- Lack of Awareness: Limited awareness and understanding of AI technologies among farmers can hinder adoption.
- Infrastructure Limitations: Inadequate infrastructure, such as lack of reliable internet connectivity, can affect the effectiveness of AI systems.

Overall Impact
Economic Impact

- Return on Investment (ROI): The benefits of AI adoption, such as increased productivity and cost savings, often outweigh the initial costs, leading to a positive ROI.
- Economic Growth: AI adoption can contribute to economic growth by boosting agricultural productivity and creating new business opportunities in the agritech sector.

Social Impact

- Improved Livelihoods: Enhanced productivity and cost savings lead to better incomes for farmers and improved livelihoods.
- Employment Opportunities: The growth of the AI and agritech sectors creates new job opportunities in technology development, support, and implementation.

Environmental Impact

- Sustainable Agriculture: AI promotes sustainable agricultural practices, contributing to environmental conservation and resilience.
- Resource Conservation: Efficient use of resources reduces the environmental footprint of farming and supports long-term sustainability.

The cost-benefit analysis of AI adoption in agriculture reveals that while the initial investment and implementation costs can be significant, the potential benefits—including increased productivity, cost savings, enhanced decision-making, risk management, and environmental sustainability—often outweigh these costs. By addressing challenges such as high initial costs, technical complexity, and data management, and by leveraging the benefits of AI, the agricultural sector can achieve significant improvements in efficiency, productivity, and sustainability.

AI's Role in Enhancing Farmer Income and Reducing Costs

Artificial Intelligence (AI) is transforming agriculture by offering tools and solutions that enhance farmer income and reduce operational costs. Through various applications and technologies, AI helps farmers improve efficiency, increase yields, and optimize resource use. Here's how AI contributes to these outcomes:

Enhancing Farmer Income

Yield Optimization

- **Precision Farming**: AI-driven precision farming techniques optimize crop management practices. By analyzing data on soil conditions, weather patterns, and crop health, AI systems recommend precise amounts of water, fertilizers, and pesticides. This leads to higher crop yields and better-quality produce, directly impacting farmer income.
- **Predictive Analytics**: AI models predict crop yields and market demand, allowing farmers to make informed decisions about crop selection and timing. Accurate yield predictions help farmers plan for optimal harvests and avoid losses, thus improving profitability.

Market Access and Pricing

- **Market Price Forecasting**: AI algorithms analyze market trends and historical data to forecast future prices. This information helps farmers make strategic decisions about when and where to sell their produce, maximizing their revenue by selling at optimal times and prices.
- **Supply Chain Management**: AI streamlines supply chains by improving logistics, reducing waste, and enhancing traceability. Efficient supply chains ensure that produce reaches markets in better condition and with minimal spoilage, increasing the overall value and income for farmers.

Risk Management

- **Disease and Pest Detection**: AI-powered systems detect diseases and pests early through image recognition and sensor data. Early detection allows for timely interventions, reducing crop losses and ensuring higher yields. This contributes to stable income for farmers by minimizing unexpected losses.
- **Weather Forecasting**: AI enhances weather forecasting accuracy, helping farmers prepare for adverse weather conditions. By predicting extreme weather events and suggesting preventive measures, AI reduces the risk of crop damage and associated income losses.

Resource Efficiency

- **Water Management**: AI optimizes irrigation systems by analyzing soil moisture levels and weather forecasts. Efficient water use not only reduces costs but also improves crop health and yields, leading to increased income.
- **Fertilizer and Pesticide Use**: AI recommendations on the precise application of fertilizers and pesticides reduce unnecessary usage, lowering input costs. This targeted approach enhances crop growth and quality, contributing to higher profits.

Reducing Costs
Operational Efficiency

- **Automation**: AI-driven automation in tasks such as planting, harvesting, and weeding reduces the need for manual labor. Automated systems and machinery increase efficiency, lower labor costs, and speed up operations.
- **Resource Optimization**: AI optimizes the use of resources like water, fertilizers, and energy. By minimizing wastage and ensuring that inputs are used effectively, AI reduces overall operational costs for farmers.

Energy and Equipment Management

- **Predictive Maintenance**: AI systems predict equipment failures and maintenance needs based on usage patterns and performance data. Timely maintenance prevents costly breakdowns and extends the lifespan of machinery, reducing repair costs.
- **Energy Efficiency**: AI optimizes energy use in farming operations by managing the energy consumption of equipment and irrigation systems. This leads to reduced energy costs and improved operational efficiency.

Labor Costs

- **Labor Savings**: AI technologies reduce the need for manual labor by automating repetitive and labor-intensive tasks. This decrease in labor requirements lowers operational expenses and allows farmers to allocate resources more effectively.

Data-Driven Insights

- **Cost Analysis**: AI provides detailed insights into the costs associated with various farming practices. By analyzing data on input usage and operational expenses, farmers can identify areas for cost reduction and optimize their farming practices.
- **Financial Forecasting**: AI models help farmers forecast financial outcomes based on different scenarios and inputs. This forecasting aids in budgeting and financial planning, ensuring better management of costs and resources.

AI plays a crucial role in enhancing farmer income and reducing costs through improved yield optimization, market access, risk management, and resource efficiency. By leveraging AI technologies, farmers can increase productivity, reduce operational expenses, and make informed decisions that boost profitability. As AI continues to advance, its potential to transform agriculture and support farmers in achieving sustainable and profitable farming practices will grow even further.

Impact on Agricultural Exports and Global Competitiveness

The integration of Artificial Intelligence (AI) in agriculture has profound implications for agricultural exports and global competitiveness. By enhancing productivity, efficiency, and quality, AI helps countries improve their position in the global agricultural market. Here's how AI impacts agricultural exports and global competitiveness:

Enhancing Export Quality and Quantity

Quality Improvement

- **Precision Agriculture**: AI technologies, such as precision farming, optimize crop management practices, resulting in higher-quality produce. By ensuring optimal use of resources and effective pest and disease management, AI helps in producing consistent and high-quality products that meet international standards.
- **Post-Harvest Processing**: AI systems in post-harvest processing, including sorting and grading, ensure that only the best quality produce reaches the export market. This quality control improves the reputation of agricultural products in global markets.

Increased Production

- **Yield Maximization**: AI-driven techniques for yield optimization, such as predictive analytics and precision irrigation, lead to higher crop yields. Increased production enhances the supply of exportable goods, allowing countries to meet global demand and expand their market share.
- **Resource Efficiency**: By optimizing the use of water, fertilizers, and pesticides, AI reduces wastage and improves overall productivity. Efficient resource use supports higher production levels, contributing to a larger exportable surplus.

Market Access and Expansion
Market Insights

- **Demand Forecasting**: AI analyzes market trends and consumer preferences to forecast demand for agricultural products. This information helps farmers and exporters target markets with the highest demand, increasing their chances of successful market entry and expansion.
- **Competitive Pricing**: AI models help in determining competitive pricing strategies based on market conditions and price forecasts. Competitive pricing enhances the attractiveness of agricultural exports in international markets.

Supply Chain Optimization

- **Logistics Management**: AI improves supply chain logistics by optimizing transportation routes, managing inventory, and reducing spoilage. Efficient supply chains ensure timely delivery of agricultural products to international markets, enhancing export performance.
- **Traceability**: AI enhances traceability and transparency in the supply chain, which is increasingly demanded by international markets. Improved traceability builds trust with international buyers and complies with global standards.

Improving Global Competitiveness
Innovation and Technology Leadership

- **Technological Advancements**: Countries that adopt AI technologies in agriculture position themselves as leaders in agricultural innovation.

Technological advancements enhance competitiveness by improving efficiency, productivity, and the ability to adapt to market changes.

- **Research and Development**: AI-driven research and development lead to the creation of new crop varieties, improved farming techniques, and innovative products. R&D investments strengthen a country's competitive edge in the global agricultural market.

Cost Efficiency

- **Reduced Production Costs**: AI optimizes resource use and automates labor-intensive tasks, leading to reduced production costs. Lower costs of production make agricultural products more competitive on the global stage.
- **Operational Efficiency**: AI-driven automation and optimization improve operational efficiency, allowing for higher output with lower input costs. Efficient operations enhance global competitiveness by enabling more competitive pricing.

Adapting to Global Trends
Sustainability and Environmental Stewardship

- **Sustainable Practices**: AI promotes sustainable agricultural practices by optimizing resource use and reducing environmental impact. Countries that adopt sustainable practices enhance their global reputation and align with international sustainability trends.
- **Climate Resilience**: AI helps in developing climate-resilient farming practices and adapting to changing environmental conditions. Resilient agricultural practices ensure stable production and competitiveness in the face of climate challenges.

Regulatory Compliance

- **Meeting Standards**: AI assists in ensuring compliance with international regulatory standards and certifications. Meeting these standards is crucial for accessing and maintaining entry into global markets.

Innovation in Export Products

- **Product Differentiation**: AI enables the development of value-added and differentiated agricultural products. Innovative products attract premium prices in international markets and enhance global competitiveness.

AI significantly impacts agricultural exports and global competitiveness by improving quality, increasing production, optimizing supply chains, and enhancing technological leadership. By leveraging AI technologies, countries can enhance their export performance, meet international market demands, and strengthen their position in the global agricultural industry. The ongoing advancements in AI will continue to drive competitiveness and open new opportunities for agricultural exports.

Job Creation and Skill Development Opportunities

The integration of Artificial Intelligence (AI) in agriculture brings substantial opportunities for job creation and skill development. As AI technologies transform farming practices, they create new roles and require a diverse set of skills, fostering economic growth and professional development within the agricultural sector.

Job Creation Opportunities

Technology Development and Support

- **AI Specialists**: The development and implementation of AI technologies in agriculture require AI specialists and data scientists. These professionals design and fine-tune algorithms, develop machine learning models, and ensure the effective use of AI tools.
- **Software Engineers**: Engineers who develop agricultural AI applications and platforms play a crucial role in creating user-friendly and effective tools for farmers.
- **Technical Support Staff**: Support roles are essential for troubleshooting, maintaining, and updating AI systems and software used in agriculture.

Field Operations

- **Precision Farming Technicians**: Technicians who manage and operate precision farming equipment, such as drones and automated tractors, are in demand. These roles involve setting up, calibrating, and maintaining advanced agricultural machinery.

- **Data Analysts**: Professionals who analyze data collected from AI systems, such as soil sensors and weather stations, provide actionable insights that help farmers make informed decisions.

Training and Education

- **Agricultural Educators**: Educators and trainers who specialize in AI and technology integration offer training programs and workshops for farmers and agricultural workers, enhancing their skills and knowledge.
- **Consultants**: Agricultural consultants who advise farmers on the adoption and effective use of AI technologies contribute to skill development and technology transfer.

Research and Development

- **R&D Professionals**: Research scientists and engineers involved in developing new AI applications and technologies for agriculture contribute to innovation and technological advancement.
- **Innovation Managers**: Managers who oversee research projects and technology adoption strategies help bridge the gap between technology development and practical application in the field.

Skill Development Opportunities
Technical Skills

- **AI and Machine Learning**: Understanding AI algorithms, machine learning techniques, and data analytics is crucial for roles related to technology development, data analysis, and system management.
- **Software and Hardware Proficiency**: Skills in software programming, hardware maintenance, and system integration are necessary for working with AI tools and agricultural machinery.

Data Management

- **Data Collection and Analysis**: Skills in collecting, managing, and analyzing large volumes of data are essential for roles involving data-driven decision-making and performance optimization.

- **Data Security**: Knowledge of data protection and cybersecurity practices ensures the secure handling of sensitive agricultural data.

Field-Specific Skills

- **Precision Agriculture Techniques**: Familiarity with precision farming techniques, such as automated irrigation and nutrient management, is important for roles related to field operations and technology implementation.
- **Remote Sensing and Imaging**: Skills in operating drones, satellite imaging systems, and remote sensing technologies are valuable for monitoring and managing crops and soil health.

Soft Skills

- **Problem-Solving**: The ability to identify and address issues related to AI systems, data analysis, and field operations is critical for success in technology-driven agricultural roles.
- **Communication**: Effective communication skills are important for interacting with stakeholders, providing technical support, and delivering training programs.

Educational Pathways
Academic Programs

- **Degree Programs**: Universities and institutions offer degree programs in fields such as agricultural technology, data science, AI, and robotics, preparing students for careers in AI-driven agriculture.
- **Certification Courses**: Specialized certification courses in AI applications, precision farming, and data analysis provide targeted skills and knowledge for professionals in the sector.

Professional Development

- **Workshops and Seminars**: Workshops and seminars on AI technologies and agricultural innovations offer ongoing learning opportunities for professionals and farmers.

- **Online Courses**: Online platforms provide accessible training in AI, data analytics, and agricultural technology, enabling continuous skill development.

AI's role in agriculture creates a range of job opportunities and necessitates skill development across various domains. From technology development and field operations to data management and education, the integration of AI generates employment and fosters professional growth. By investing in education and training, individuals can acquire the skills needed to thrive in the evolving agricultural landscape, while the sector benefits from enhanced innovation, efficiency, and economic growth.

Summary Of Key Insights

Summary of Key Insights

The integration of Artificial Intelligence (AI) in agriculture is revolutionizing the sector, offering significant benefits across various domains. Here's a summary of the key insights:

Enhanced Productivity and Efficiency

- **Precision Farming**: AI enables precise management of crops by optimizing the use of resources such as water, fertilizers, and pesticides, leading to increased yields and better-quality produce.
- **Data-Driven Decision Making**: AI-driven data analytics and machine learning models provide valuable insights into crop management, weather patterns, and soil health, helping farmers make informed decisions and improve productivity.

Economic and Financial Impact

- **Cost Reduction**: AI helps in reducing operational costs through automation and efficient resource management. Technologies like predictive maintenance and optimized irrigation systems lower production expenses.
- **Increased Income**: By improving yield predictions, market access, and quality control, AI contributes to higher farmer incomes. AI also aids in market price forecasting and competitive pricing strategies, enhancing profitability.

Global Competitiveness

- **Export Quality and Quantity**: AI enhances the quality of agricultural products and increases production, improving a country's position in the global market. Efficient supply chains and traceability boost export performance.
- **Technological Leadership**: Countries adopting AI in agriculture gain a competitive edge through innovation and technological advancements, strengthening their global standing.

Job Creation and Skill Development

- **New Roles**: The rise of AI in agriculture creates job opportunities in areas such as AI development, data analysis, precision farming, and technical support.
- **Skill Requirements**: There is a growing need for skills in AI, machine learning, data management, and precision agriculture. Educational programs and professional training are essential for developing a skilled workforce.

Challenges and Barriers

- **Technological Barriers**: Limited infrastructure, connectivity issues, and high costs of technology adoption pose challenges to the widespread implementation of AI in agriculture.
- **Economic Constraints**: Financial limitations and high initial investments in AI technologies can be significant barriers for smallholder farmers and developing regions.

Future Prospects

- **Emerging Trends**: Advancements in AI technologies, such as AI for climate-resilient agriculture and sustainable farming practices, hold promise for further enhancing agricultural productivity and sustainability.
- **Policy and Collaboration**: Effective policies, government initiatives, and public-private partnerships are crucial for supporting AI adoption in agriculture. International cooperation and knowledge sharing also play a vital role in advancing AI-driven solutions.

Ethical and Environmental Considerations

- **Sustainability**: AI can promote sustainable farming practices and climate resilience, aligning with global trends towards environmental stewardship.
- **Ethical Issues**: Addressing ethical concerns related to data privacy, equity in technology access, and environmental impacts is essential for the responsible deployment of AI in agriculture.

AI is transforming agriculture by enhancing productivity, reducing costs, and improving global competitiveness. It creates new job opportunities and requires a diverse set of skills, while also presenting challenges that need to be addressed. The future of AI in agriculture holds great promise for innovation, sustainability, and economic growth, provided that supportive policies, collaboration, and ethical considerations are effectively managed.

The Future Landscape Of Ai In Indian Agriculture

The Future Landscape of AI in Indian Agriculture

The future of AI in Indian agriculture promises transformative changes, driven by advancements in technology, evolving needs of the agricultural sector, and supportive policy frameworks. As AI technologies continue to evolve, their integration into Indian agriculture is expected to enhance productivity, sustainability, and resilience. Here's an overview of the potential future landscape of AI in Indian agriculture:

1. Advancements in Technology

- **Enhanced Precision Farming**: Future developments in AI will lead to even more refined precision farming techniques. Advanced sensors, drones, and satellite imaging will provide detailed insights into soil health, crop conditions, and resource needs, allowing for hyper-localized and optimized farming practices.
- **Integration of AI with IoT**: The convergence of AI and the Internet of Things (IoT) will facilitate real-time monitoring and automation. Smart sensors and connected devices will enable continuous data collection and analysis, improving decision-making and operational efficiency.
- **Machine Learning Innovations**: As machine learning algorithms become more sophisticated, they will offer deeper insights into crop management, pest control, and yield prediction. AI systems will become better at forecasting and adapting to changing environmental conditions and market trends.

2. Sustainable and Climate-Resilient Agriculture

- **Climate Adaptation**: AI will play a crucial role in developing climate-resilient agricultural practices. Predictive models and simulations will help farmers anticipate and mitigate the effects of climate change, such as extreme weather events and shifting growing seasons.
- **Resource Efficiency**: Future AI technologies will further enhance resource efficiency, reducing water and fertilizer usage while minimizing environmental impact. Sustainable practices promoted by AI will support the goals of environmental conservation and soil health.
- **Organic Farming Integration**: AI will support organic and sustainable

farming practices by optimizing natural inputs and managing organic pest control methods. AI tools will assist in maintaining soil health and enhancing biodiversity.

3. Expansion of AI Applications

- **Advanced Pest and Disease Management**: AI will enable more accurate and timely detection of pests and diseases through image recognition and pattern analysis. Automated intervention systems, such as AI-driven sprayers and targeted treatments, will improve crop protection.
- **Smart Irrigation Systems**: AI-powered smart irrigation systems will use real-time data on weather conditions, soil moisture, and crop requirements to optimize water use. These systems will reduce water wastage and ensure precise irrigation.
- **Automated Harvesting and Processing**: Robotics and AI will advance automated harvesting and post-harvest processing. Robotics will handle tasks such as picking, sorting, and packing, increasing efficiency and reducing labor costs.

4. Enhancing Farmer Support and Education

- **AI-Powered Advisory Services**: AI-driven advisory platforms will provide personalized recommendations and guidance to farmers. These platforms will offer insights on best practices, weather forecasts, and market trends, empowering farmers with knowledge and support.
- **Training and Capacity Building**: The expansion of AI in agriculture will necessitate widespread training and education programs. Skill development initiatives will focus on equipping farmers and agricultural workers with the knowledge to effectively use AI tools and technologies.

5. Policy and Infrastructure Development

- **Supportive Policies**: Future policies will need to address the regulatory, financial, and infrastructural challenges associated with AI adoption. Supportive measures, including subsidies, grants, and incentives, will encourage technology adoption and innovation.
- **Infrastructure Enhancement**: Improved infrastructure, such as high-speed internet and robust data management systems, will be essential

for the effective implementation of AI technologies in rural and remote areas.

6. Ethical and Social Considerations

- **Data Privacy and Security**: Ensuring data privacy and security will be critical as AI systems collect and analyze large volumes of agricultural data. Transparent practices and robust data protection measures will be necessary to address concerns.
- **Equity and Access**: Addressing disparities in access to AI technologies will be important for ensuring that smallholder farmers and marginalized communities benefit from advancements in agriculture. Inclusive policies and programs will promote equitable technology access.

7. Collaborative Efforts and Global Integration

- **Public-Private Partnerships**: Collaboration between government agencies, private companies, and research institutions will drive innovation and implementation of AI in agriculture. Partnerships will facilitate knowledge sharing, technology development, and scaling of successful solutions.
- **International Cooperation**: Global cooperation and exchange of best practices will enhance AI applications in Indian agriculture. Engagement with international research communities and organizations will support the adoption of cutting-edge technologies and methodologies.

The future landscape of AI in Indian agriculture holds great promise for enhancing productivity, sustainability, and resilience. With advancements in technology, supportive policies, and collaborative efforts, AI will transform agricultural practices, address challenges, and open new opportunities for growth. As AI continues to evolve, its integration into Indian agriculture will play a pivotal role in shaping a more efficient, sustainable, and prosperous agricultural sector.

Vision For 2030: Ai Transforming Indian Agriculture

Vision for 2030: AI Transforming Indian Agriculture

By 2030, AI is poised to play a transformative role in Indian agriculture, revolutionizing the sector through advanced technologies, enhanced sustainability, and improved economic outcomes. The vision for 2030 encompasses several key areas where AI will make a significant impact:

1. Precision Farming and Resource Management

- **Hyper-Local Precision**: AI will enable hyper-local precision farming, with advanced sensors and AI algorithms providing detailed, real-time data on soil conditions, crop health, and environmental factors. This will allow for highly targeted interventions, optimizing the use of water, fertilizers, and pesticides to maximize yield and minimize waste.
- **Automated Resource Management**: AI-driven systems will manage irrigation, fertilization, and pest control automatically, based on real-time data. Smart irrigation systems will use weather forecasts, soil moisture levels, and crop needs to deliver precise amounts of water, reducing wastage and improving efficiency.

2. Climate Resilience and Sustainable Practices

- **Climate-Resilient Crops**: AI will help develop and manage climate-resilient crop varieties that can withstand extreme weather conditions and adapt to changing climates. Predictive models will guide breeding programs and help farmers select the best crop varieties for their specific conditions.
- **Sustainable Agriculture**: AI will support sustainable farming practices by optimizing resource use, reducing the environmental impact of farming, and promoting practices such as conservation tillage and organic farming. AI systems will monitor and manage soil health, enhance biodiversity, and reduce carbon footprints.

3. Advanced Crop and Soil Monitoring

- **Real-Time Monitoring**: AI will provide real-time monitoring of crop health and soil conditions using drones, satellites, and ground-based sensors. This will enable early detection of issues such as nutrient deficiencies, diseases, and pests, allowing for timely and effective interventions.

- **Soil Health Management**: AI will analyze soil data to provide insights into soil fertility, structure, and composition. This will guide farmers in making informed decisions about soil management practices, including crop rotation and organic amendments.

4. Automation and Robotics

- **Automated Harvesting**: Robotics and AI will advance automated harvesting systems, capable of efficiently picking, sorting, and packing crops. These systems will reduce labor costs, increase harvest efficiency, and improve the quality of harvested produce.
- **Precision Agriculture Robots**: Autonomous robots equipped with AI will perform tasks such as planting, weeding, and pruning with high precision. These robots will work alongside farmers, enhancing productivity and reducing the physical labor required.

5. Farmer Support and Advisory Services

- **AI-Powered Advisory Systems**: AI-driven advisory platforms will provide farmers with personalized recommendations based on data from their fields. These platforms will offer insights on best practices, weather forecasts, market trends, and financial planning, empowering farmers to make informed decisions.
- **Education and Training**: AI will facilitate widespread training and education programs, equipping farmers with the skills needed to utilize advanced technologies effectively. Online platforms and mobile applications will offer accessible training resources and support.

6. Economic and Market Insights

- **Yield Prediction and Market Forecasting**: AI will enhance yield prediction models, providing accurate forecasts of crop production and market demand. This will help farmers plan their production and marketing strategies more effectively, reducing financial risk.
- **Supply Chain Optimization**: AI will streamline supply chain

management, from farm to market. Blockchain technology and AI will ensure transparency, traceability, and efficiency in the agricultural supply chain, reducing costs and improving market access.

7. Policy and Infrastructure Development

- **Supportive Policies**: Governments will implement policies that support the adoption of AI in agriculture, including subsidies, grants, and incentives. These policies will encourage technology adoption and foster innovation in the sector.
- **Infrastructure Enhancements**: Investments in infrastructure, such as high-speed internet and data management systems, will be critical for the widespread implementation of AI technologies. Improved connectivity will enable farmers in remote areas to access AI-driven tools and services.

8. Ethical and Inclusive Growth

- **Data Privacy and Security**: Ensuring data privacy and security will be a priority as AI systems collect and analyze agricultural data. Transparent practices and robust protection measures will address concerns and build trust among stakeholders.
- **Equitable Access**: Efforts will be made to ensure that smallholder farmers and marginalized communities benefit from AI advancements. Inclusive policies and programs will promote equitable access to technology and support for underserved regions.

By 2030, AI will fundamentally transform Indian agriculture, driving innovation, sustainability, and efficiency. The vision for the future includes enhanced precision farming, climate resilience, advanced monitoring, automation, and comprehensive farmer support. Through supportive policies, infrastructure development, and a focus on ethical and inclusive growth, AI will play a pivotal role in shaping a prosperous and sustainable agricultural sector in India.

Final Thoughts And Call To Action

Final Thoughts and Call to Action

As we look toward the future of agriculture in India, the integration of Artificial Intelligence (AI) presents a remarkable opportunity to address longstanding challenges and drive transformative change. The potential of AI to enhance productivity, sustainability, and economic viability in agriculture is immense, but realizing this potential requires collective effort and strategic planning.

Final Thoughts

1. Embracing Innovation: AI is not just a technological advancement but a critical tool for the evolution of agriculture. It offers solutions to some of the most pressing issues facing the sector, such as resource scarcity, climate change, and the need for increased productivity. Embracing AI can lead to smarter farming practices, more efficient use of resources, and improved crop and livestock management.

2. Addressing Challenges: While the benefits of AI are significant, there are challenges to overcome, including technological barriers, financial constraints, and the need for widespread education and training. It is crucial to address these challenges through supportive policies, investment in infrastructure, and targeted training programs to ensure that all stakeholders can effectively harness the power of AI.

3. Ethical and Inclusive Approach: The deployment of AI in agriculture must be guided by ethical considerations and a commitment to inclusivity. Ensuring data privacy, equitable access to technology, and addressing environmental impacts are essential to fostering a responsible and sustainable integration of AI in agriculture.

4. Collaborative Efforts: The successful adoption and implementation of AI in agriculture will require collaboration between government agencies, private sector companies, research institutions, and farmers. Public-private partnerships, international cooperation, and community engagement will be key to driving innovation and achieving widespread impact.

Call to Action

1. Invest in Technology and Infrastructure: Stakeholders should prioritize investments in AI technologies and the necessary infrastructure to support their deployment. This includes improving connectivity, enhancing data management systems, and developing cutting-edge AI tools tailored to the needs of Indian agriculture.

2. Support Research and Development: Encourage and fund research initiatives focused on AI applications in agriculture. This will help advance the technology, address specific challenges, and develop solutions that are well-suited to the diverse agricultural landscapes and practices in India.

3. Promote Education and Training: Develop and implement training programs to educate farmers, agricultural workers, and industry professionals about AI technologies. Provide accessible resources and support to ensure that all stakeholders can effectively utilize AI tools and benefit from their capabilities.

4. Foster Collaboration and Partnerships: Build and strengthen partnerships between government, private sector, academic institutions, and farmer organizations. Collaborative efforts will drive innovation, facilitate knowledge sharing, and support the scaling of successful AI solutions across the agricultural sector.

5. Advocate for Supportive Policies: Advocate for policies and regulations that support the adoption of AI in agriculture. This includes providing incentives, subsidies, and grants to encourage technology adoption, as well as developing frameworks that address ethical concerns and promote inclusive growth.

6. Focus on Sustainable Practices: Ensure that AI applications in agriculture are aligned with sustainability goals. Promote practices that enhance environmental stewardship, reduce resource waste, and support climate resilience.

7. Engage in Global Knowledge Sharing: Participate in international forums, conferences, and collaborations to stay abreast of global advancements in AI and agriculture. Sharing knowledge and best practices will contribute to the development of innovative solutions and foster global cooperation.

Conclusion

The future of Indian agriculture is ripe with potential, and AI stands as a powerful catalyst for transformation. By taking proactive steps to embrace innovation, address challenges, and foster collaboration, we can unlock the full potential of AI and build a more productive, sustainable, and resilient agricultural sector. The time to act is now—together, we can shape the future of agriculture and ensure a prosperous future for farmers and communities across India.

Glossary Of Ai And Agricultural Terms

Artificial Intelligence (AI): A branch of computer science focused on creating systems capable of performing tasks that normally require human intelligence, such as learning, reasoning, and problem-solving.

Machine Learning (ML): A subset of AI involving algorithms and statistical models that enable computers to improve their performance on tasks through experience and data, without being explicitly programmed.

Deep Learning: A specialized area of machine learning that uses neural networks with many layers (deep networks) to analyze complex patterns in large datasets, such as images or text.

Neural Networks: Computing systems inspired by the human brain's network of neurons, used in deep learning to recognize patterns and make predictions based on data.

Internet of Things (IoT): A network of interconnected devices and sensors that collect, transmit, and receive data over the internet, enabling smart and automated systems.

Precision Farming: An agricultural management concept using technology to observe, measure, and respond to variability in crops and soil, aiming to optimize resource use and improve crop yield.

Smart Sensors: Devices that collect data from the environment or crops, such as temperature, humidity, or soil moisture, and transmit this information for analysis and decision-making.

Robotics: The design and use of robots to perform tasks autonomously or semi-autonomously, including planting, harvesting, and monitoring crops.

Drones: Unmanned aerial vehicles (UAVs) equipped with cameras and sensors used for aerial monitoring, imaging, and data collection in agriculture.

Satellite Imaging: The use of satellites to capture images and data about the Earth's surface, providing valuable information on crop health, soil conditions, and land use.

Blockchain: A decentralized digital ledger technology used to record transactions across a network of computers, ensuring transparency, security, and traceability in supply chains.

Yield Prediction: The process of forecasting the amount of crop that will be harvested based on various factors such as weather, soil conditions, and crop management practices.

Precision Irrigation: The use of technology to deliver precise amounts of water to crops based on real-time data, improving water use efficiency and reducing wastage.

Climate Resilience: The ability of agricultural systems to withstand and adapt to the effects of climate change, such as extreme weather events and shifting growing conditions.

Soil Health Monitoring: The assessment of soil conditions, including nutrient levels, pH, and organic matter, to manage soil fertility and optimize crop growth.

Pest Detection: The use of technology, such as image recognition and sensor data, to identify and monitor pests and diseases affecting crops.

Disease Management: Strategies and technologies used to prevent, detect, and control plant diseases to minimize crop losses and maintain yield.

Agricultural Supply Chain: The series of steps involved in producing, processing, and distributing agricultural products from farms to consumers, including production, processing, packaging, and transportation.

Decision Support Systems (DSS): Computer-based systems that analyze data and provide recommendations to assist farmers in making informed decisions about crop management, resource use, and market strategies.

Bioinoculants: Microorganisms used to enhance plant growth and soil health, such as bacteria and fungi that promote nutrient uptake and improve soil fertility.

Agroecology: A holistic approach to farming that integrates ecological principles into agricultural practices, focusing on sustainability, biodiversity, and the efficient use of resources.

Data Analytics: The process of examining large datasets to uncover patterns, trends, and insights that inform decision-making and strategic planning.

AI-Driven Advisory Systems: Platforms that use AI algorithms to provide personalized recommendations and guidance to farmers, based on data from their fields and external sources.

Economic Viability: The ability of a farming practice or technology to be financially sustainable, considering costs, benefits, and returns on investment.

Public-Private Partnerships (PPPs): Collaborations between government entities and private sector organizations to achieve common goals, such as advancing technology and supporting agricultural development.

Smart Farming: An approach that integrates modern technologies, such as AI, IoT, and robotics, to optimize farming practices, improve efficiency, and increase productivity.

AgTech: Technology solutions specifically designed for the agricultural sector, including innovations in AI, robotics, data analytics, and automation.

Crop Management: The practices and technologies used to optimize crop growth, yield, and quality, including planting, fertilization, irrigation, and pest control.

Farm Management Systems (FMS): Comprehensive software solutions that help farmers plan, monitor, and manage various aspects of farm operations, including crop planning, resource allocation, and financial management.

List Of Ai Tools And Technologies Used In Agriculture

? **Drone Technology**: Unmanned aerial vehicles equipped with cameras and sensors used for aerial imaging, crop monitoring, and data collection. Drones help in assessing crop health, mapping fields, and detecting issues such as pest infestations and nutrient deficiencies.

? **Satellite Imagery**: High-resolution images captured by satellites used for monitoring large areas of farmland. Satellite data provides insights into crop health, soil conditions, and weather patterns, aiding in precision farming and yield prediction.

? **AI-Powered Crop Monitoring Systems**: Tools that utilize AI algorithms to analyze data from sensors, drones, and satellites to monitor crop health, growth stages, and detect diseases and pests.

? **Precision Irrigation Systems**: Automated irrigation systems that use AI to optimize water usage based on real-time data from soil moisture sensors, weather forecasts, and crop needs.

? **Robotic Harvesters**: Autonomous robots designed for harvesting crops with high precision and efficiency. These robots can identify and pick ripe fruits or vegetables, reducing labor costs and improving harvest quality.

? **AI-Based Soil Health Monitors**: Systems that use sensors and AI to analyze soil properties such as nutrient levels, pH, and moisture content. These tools provide recommendations for soil management and fertilization.

? **Predictive Analytics Platforms**: AI tools that forecast crop yields, market prices, and weather patterns based on historical data and real-time inputs. These platforms help farmers make informed decisions about planting, harvesting, and marketing.

? **Pest and Disease Detection Systems**: AI-driven solutions that use image recognition and machine learning to identify pests and diseases affecting crops. These systems can analyze photos from drones or smartphones to provide early warnings and treatment recommendations.

? **Farm Management Software**: Comprehensive platforms that integrate AI to manage various aspects of farm operations, including crop planning, resource allocation, financial management, and decision support.

? **AI-Powered Advisory Services**: Digital platforms that provide farmers with personalized recommendations based on data from their fields, including advice on crop management, pest control, and resource optimization.

? **Automated Weeding Systems**: Robots and machines equipped with AI that can identify and remove weeds from fields with precision, reducing the need for manual labor and chemical herbicides.

? **Yield Prediction Models**: AI algorithms that analyze historical and real-time data to predict crop yields. These models use factors such as weather, soil conditions, and crop management practices to provide accurate forecasts.

? **Blockchain-Based Supply Chain Solutions**: AI-enhanced blockchain systems that ensure transparency, traceability, and efficiency in the agricultural supply chain, from production to distribution.

? **Smart Sensors for Environmental Monitoring**: IoT sensors that collect data on environmental conditions such as temperature, humidity, and soil moisture. AI analyzes this data to provide insights and recommendations for optimizing crop growth.

? **Livestock Monitoring Systems**: AI-powered tools that track the health, behavior, and productivity of livestock. These systems use sensors and machine learning to monitor vital signs, detect illnesses, and optimize feeding practices.

? **Automated Planting Systems**: Robotics and AI systems that perform planting tasks with high precision, including seed placement, depth control, and spacing. These systems improve planting efficiency and consistency.

? **Climate and Weather Forecasting Tools**: AI tools that provide detailed and accurate weather forecasts for agricultural planning. These tools use data from weather stations, satellites, and other sources to predict weather patterns and help farmers make informed decisions.

References And Further Reading

Books and Reports

- **"Artificial Intelligence in Agriculture: A Review"** - K. Naik, et al. (2020). This comprehensive review explores various applications of AI in agriculture and provides insights into the current advancements and challenges.
- **"Precision Agriculture for Sustainability and Environmental Protection"** - J. Stafford (2021). This book discusses the integration of AI and precision agriculture to enhance sustainability and environmental stewardship in farming.
- **"The Future of Farming: How AI and Technology are Transforming Agriculture"** - R. Brown and S. Smith (2022). This book provides an overview of the latest technological advancements in agriculture, including AI-driven innovations.
- **"AI in Agriculture: Challenges and Opportunities"** - P. Kumar and A. Singh (2021). This report covers the current state of AI in agriculture, discussing both the challenges and potential opportunities for growth.

Academic Journals

- **"Journal of Artificial Intelligence Research"** - Provides research articles and reviews on various AI applications, including those in agriculture.
- **"Computers and Electronics in Agriculture"** - This journal features research on the integration of computers, electronics, and AI in agricultural practices.
- **"Precision Agriculture"** - Focuses on advancements in precision farming technologies and their impact on agricultural productivity and sustainability.
- **"International Journal of Agricultural and Biological Engineering"** - Publishes research on the application of engineering and AI technologies in agriculture.

Websites and Online Resources

- **Agricultural Robotics Research Center (ARRC)** - ARRC Website: A resource for information on the latest developments in agricultural robotics and AI.

- **International Food Policy Research Institute (IFPRI)** - IFPRI Website: Provides reports and research on agricultural innovations, including AI applications.
- **AgFunder Network Partners** - AgFunder Website: Offers insights into the role of startups and investments in agricultural technology, including AI solutions.
- **World Bank Agriculture and Rural Development** - World Bank Website: Features reports and publications on agricultural development and technological advancements.
- **AI in Agriculture Blog by IBM** - IBM Blog: Provides articles and updates on how IBM's AI technologies are being applied in agriculture.

Research Papers and Articles

- "**Applications of Machine Learning in Agriculture: A Review**" - J. Ghosh and R. Kumar (2022). A detailed review of machine learning techniques applied to various agricultural problems.
- "**Impact of AI on Agricultural Productivity: A Meta-Analysis**" - L. Zhang, et al. (2023). Analyzes the effects of AI adoption on crop yield and farming efficiency through a meta-analysis of existing studies.
- "**Smart Farming and AI: Current Trends and Future Directions**" - N. Patel and M. Sharma (2021). Discusses the latest trends in smart farming and the role of AI in shaping future agricultural practices.

Online Courses and Webinars

- **Coursera: "AI for Everyone"** by Andrew Ng - Coursera Course: Provides a foundational understanding of AI, which can be applied to various fields, including agriculture.
- **edX: "Data Science and Machine Learning for Agriculture"** - edX Course: An online course focusing on the application of data science and machine learning in agriculture.
- **Webinar Series by the Agricultural Technology Research Association (ATRA)** - ATRA Webinars: Offers webinars on the latest technological advancements and research in agricultural technology.

List Of Key Organizations And Startups In Ai And Agriculture

Organizations

- **International Food Policy Research Institute (IFPRI):** http://www.ifpri.org
- **Food and Agriculture Organization (FAO):** http://www.fao.org
- **World Bank Agriculture and Rural Development:** http://www.worldbank.org/en/topic/agriculture
- **International Rice Research Institute (IRRI):** http://www.irri.org
- **International Crops Research Institute for the Semi-Arid Tropics (ICRISAT):** http://www.icrisat.org

Startups

- **AgroStar:** http://www.agrostar.in
- **CropIn Technology Solutions:** http://www.cropin.com
- **Taranis:** http://www.taranis.ag
- **FarmLogs:** http://www.farmlogs.com
- **Prospera Technologies:** http://www.prospera.ag
- **XAG:** http://www.xa.com
- **AgBiome:** http://www.agbiome.com
- **Aker Technologies:** http://www.akertech.com
- **Resson:** http://www.resson.com
- **S4 Agriculture:** http://www.s4agriculture.com
- **AgEagle:** http://www.ageagle.com
- **Hello Tractor:** http://www.hellotractor.com
- **AquaSpy:** http://www.aquaspy.com

These organizations and startups are key players in integrating AI technologies into agriculture, offering various solutions to enhance productivity, sustainability, and efficiency in farming practices.

Questionnaires And Surveys Used In Research

Designing Effective Questionnaires and Surveys

1. **Purpose and Objectives:**

   - Clearly define the research objectives and what information is needed.
   - Ensure that the questions align with these objectives to gather relevant data.

2. **Question Types:**

   - **Closed-Ended Questions**: Provide specific options for respondents to choose from (e.g., multiple-choice, Likert scale).
   - **Open-Ended Questions**: Allow respondents to answer in their own words, providing more detailed and qualitative insights.
   - **Ranking Questions**: Ask respondents to rank items based on preference or importance.
   - **Likert Scale Questions**: Measure attitudes or opinions on a scale (e.g., strongly agree to strongly disagree).

3. **Questionnaire Structure:**

   - **Introduction**: Briefly explain the purpose of the survey and how the data will be used.
   - **Demographic Information**: Collect basic information about respondents (e.g., age, gender, occupation).
   - **Main Questions**: Focus on the core research topics. Group related questions together to maintain logical flow.
   - **Closing**: Thank respondents and provide any necessary follow-up instructions.

4. **Survey Design Considerations:**

   - **Clarity**: Ensure questions are clear and easily understandable to avoid confusion.

- ◦ **Brevity**: Keep the survey concise to maintain respondent engagement and reduce drop-off rates.
- ◦ **Neutral Wording**: Avoid leading or biased questions to ensure unbiased responses.

5. **Pilot Testing**:

- ◦ Conduct a pilot test with a small group to identify any issues with question clarity, structure, or response options.

6. **Distribution Methods**:

- ◦ **Online Surveys**: Use platforms like SurveyMonkey, Google Forms, or Qualtrics for digital distribution.
- ◦ **Paper Surveys**: Distribute physical copies for in-person completion.
- ◦ **Telephone Surveys**: Conduct interviews over the phone for more personalized data collection.

Examples of Questionnaires and Surveys

1. **Agricultural Practices Survey**:

- ◦ **Objective**: To assess current farming practices and technology adoption among farmers.
- ◦ **Sample Questions**:

    - What type of crops do you primarily grow?
    - Have you adopted any modern technologies (e.g., AI, drones) in your farming practices?
    - How satisfied are you with the current technology you use? (Likert scale)
    - What are the biggest challenges you face in your farming operations?

2. **AI Technology Adoption Questionnaire**:

- ◦ **Objective**: To evaluate the adoption and impact of AI technologies in agriculture.

- ◦ **Sample Questions**:

  - Which AI technologies have you implemented in your farm operations? (Check all that apply)
  - What benefits have you experienced from using AI technologies? (e.g., increased yield, cost reduction)
  - What barriers have you encountered in adopting AI technologies? (Open-ended)
  - How likely are you to invest in additional AI solutions in the next year? (Likert scale)

3. **Farmer Training and Education Survey**:

   - ◦ **Objective**: To understand the training needs and educational gaps among farmers regarding AI and technology.
   - ◦ **Sample Questions**:

     - What types of training have you received related to modern agricultural technologies?
     - How effective was the training in improving your understanding of these technologies? (Likert scale)
     - What additional training or resources would help you better utilize AI in your farming practices?
     - Are there specific areas where you feel more education is needed?

4. **Impact of AI on Crop Yield Survey**:

   - ◦ **Objective**: To measure the impact of AI applications on crop yield and productivity.
   - ◦ **Sample Questions**:

     - How has the use of AI technologies affected your crop yield over the past year? (e.g., increased, decreased, no change)
     - What specific AI applications have contributed most to changes in crop yield? (e.g., precision irrigation, pest detection)
     - Have you noticed any improvements in crop quality as a result of using AI technologies? (Yes/No, with additional comments)
     - How would you rate the overall impact of AI on your farming

operations? (Likert scale)

5. **Livestock Management and Health Monitoring Survey:**

- **Objective:** To explore the use of AI in managing livestock health and productivity.
- **Sample Questions:**

  - What AI tools do you use for livestock management? (e.g., health monitoring, feeding optimization)
  - How has AI improved your ability to monitor livestock health and productivity? (Likert scale)
  - What challenges have you faced in implementing AI solutions for livestock management? (Open-ended)
  - How do you assess the cost-effectiveness of AI technologies in livestock management?

These questionnaires and surveys can be adapted and tailored based on specific research needs, providing valuable insights into the application and impact of AI technologies in agriculture.